States of Mind
A Study of Anglo-Irish Conflict 1780–1980

States of Mind

*A Study of Anglo-Irish Conflict
1780–1980*

OLIVER MACDONAGH

London
GEORGE ALLEN & UNWIN
Boston   Sydney

George Allen & Unwin (Publishers) Ltd,
40 Museum Street, London WC1A 1LU, UK

George Allen & Unwin (Publishers) Ltd,
Park Lane, Hemel Hempstead, Herts HP2 4TE, UK

Allen & Unwin, Inc.,
9 Winchester Terrace, Winchester, Mass. 01890, USA

George Allen & Unwin Australia Pty Ltd,
8 Napier Street, North Sydney, NSW 2060, Australia

First paperback edition 1985

British Library Cataloguing in Publication Data

MacDonagh, Oliver
    States of mind: a study of Anglo-Irish conflict.
1. Ireland—Politics and government—19th century
2. Ireland—Politics and government—20th century
3. Ireland—Politics and government—1760–1820
I. Title
941.5081   DA950
ISBN 0–04–941012–1
0–04–941015–6 Pbk

Library of Congress Cataloging in Publication Data

MacDonagh, Oliver.
    States of mind.
Bibliography: p.
Includes index.
1. Ireland—Politics and government—19th century.
2. Ireland—Politics and government—20th century.
3. Great Britain—Foreign relations—Ireland.
4. Ireland—Foreign relations—Great Britain.
5. Irish question.
I. Title.
DA950.M184   1983   941.508   83–6427
ISBN 0–04–941012–1
0–04–941015–6 Pbk

Set in 10 on 11 point Plantin by Inforum Ltd, Portsmouth
and printed in Great Britain
Anchor Brendon Limited, Tiptree, Essex

Contents

*For Pat and Donagh
in memory of our childhood*

Preface

'There is a foolish opinion prevalent', Shaw once wrote, in a character-istically lengthy foreword, 'that an author should allow his works to speak for themselves'. I cannot agree that the opinion is foolish, at any rate in such a case as this. There is no conceivable pattern or template for an attempt to explore people's states of mind over two hundred years. The book's title will have to stand as its own explanation.

Similarly, its scale must stand as the justification – such as it is – of the manifold omissions and elisions. I, at least, can see no limit to the operative images and phrases, the crosspurposes and double-meanings, or the facets of evasion, ambiguity, ambivalence, dualism and other- and self-deception, in the politics of national and cultural conflict. It is wildly unlikely that anybody else, given a choice of, say, eight facets (for this was more or less my word-constraint), would have duplicated my selec-tion. Still less is it likely that any other would have been expansive wherever I expanded, and concentrated where I contracted, or made the same decisions about the genre to use for particular chapters or the most effective evidence or illustration for this point or that. In short, it was in the very nature of the enterprise to be idiosyncratic and eclectic. It must stand or fall by people's judgement of the performance, by their feeling – or otherwise – that it has exposed some hidden or half-hidden truths.

Of course, a work dedicated to thinking about history rather than to history simple draws heavily upon earlier scholarship, both *en masse* and in numerous individual instances. My debts, both general and particu-lar, are great. Some of the very largest are acknowledged in the refer-ences. But the largest of all must be specified here. Dr Barbara Solow and Dr T. J. Dunne were kind enough to furnish me with copies of their then unpublished papers, 'A New Look at the Irish Land Question' and 'Theobald Wolfe Tone: Colonial Outsider'; and Miss Margaret O'Callaghan allowed me to read her Master's dissertation, 'Land and Religion: the Quest for Identity in the Irish Free State, 1922–32'. I have used all three of them extensively, for matter and insights alike.

I am also my own shameless debtor. I have drawn freely on material which I have published in the past – once or twice, indeed, with some tacit change of mind. Again, I must particularise for especially heavy borrowings. I am very grateful to the editors of *Anglo-Irish Studies* and *Historical Studies* respectively for permission to reproduce substantial portions of my articles, 'Time's Revenges and Revenge's Time: a View of Anglo-Irish Relations' (1979) and 'Ambiguity in Nationalism: the Case of Ireland' (1981).

My old friend–censors, Dr A. W. Martin and Dr F. B. Smith of the Department of History at the Institute of Advanced Studies, Canberra, have once again saved me from various solecisms, obscurities and other works of the writer's devil; and Dr J. B. O'Brien and Dr T. J. Dunne of University College, Cork, have criticised my chapters both acutely and sympathetically. But encouragement is as important as correction to the flagging, doubting author; and here Dr Dunne's faith in the eventual outcome was of very special value, for his was the faith of a true believer in the practically unworked field of the history of ideas and mentality in Ireland.

There are other debts. I acknowledge warmly the opportunity for writing – as well as much personal kindness – provided by the Master and Fellows of St John's College, Cambridge, when they elected me Overseas Scholar for the Michaelmas term 1981. I must also express my keen appreciation of the work of the departmental staff, Janice Aldridge, Anthea Bundock, Beverly Gallina and Helen Macnab. They bore patiently with my second, third and even fourth thoughts in the course of drafting, and cheerfully responded to every unreasonable prayer. What I owe my wife is, as always, as different in depth as it is in kind from all the rest.

Canberra   O. MacD.
November 1982

Chapter 1

Time

I

After Lloyd George's first meeting with de Valera on 14 July 1921 to negotiate a peace treaty between Great Britain and Ireland, he told his secretary, 'I made no impression. I listened to a long lecture on the wrong done to Ireland . . . [by] Cromwell, and when[ever] I tried to bring him [de Valera] to the present day, back he went to Cromwell again'.[1] The trouble, as Lloyd George was saying in effect, was that while the English do not remember any history, the Irish forget none. Behind this familiar facetiousness lies a profound truth. To Lloyd George, the seventeenth century was dead, irrelevant to current difficulties, except perhaps in helping to explain how they might, remotely, have come into being. To de Valera, the seventeenth century lived on in that it had generated still unexpiated and irredeemed injustices; the mere intervention of years, however many, could do nothing whatever to change the ethical reality. When and how did this Irish habit of historical thought arise?

II

Modern Irish historiography was born in 1790 with the publication of the Revd Edward Ledwich's *Antiquities of Ireland*. Ostensibly, Ledwich wrote as an enlightenment man, bent on dissipating by eighteenth-century sunlight what he called the bardic fictions which had enveloped early Irish history. In fact, as the subsequent controversy about his work revealed, he was signalling the fact that the Irish past had become an additional arena for current Irish political conflict. His real target was rising papists like Charles O'Connor and Thomas Wyse, founders of the Catholic Committee in 1760, who had combined agitation for Catholic relief with attempts to preserve the traditional Gaelic culture. The Celtic revival had been common ground between the new Catholic intelligentsia and many of the Anglo-Irish liberals in the 1770s and 1780s, as the very warm encouragement of Celtic studies by the Royal Irish Academy in the latter decade testifies. But, consciously or unconsciously, men like O'Connor and Wyse had further ends in view than mere scholarship and the classification of antiquities. They were using the remote past to support their claims to social and civic parity. As with so many anti-colonialists of the twentieth century, they were pressing the fact and character of a pre-conquestal native civilisation into service as a means of establishing their equality of footing with their overlords. Part of the conquerors' claim to superiority rested on their supposedly more advanced culture. In so far as the gap between this and the social forms it attempted to supersede could be narrowed, *pro tanto* their ascendancy was weakened. Ledwich, however, thought that he had seen through the upstarts' design in canvassing pre-conquest Ireland. He was not deceived as to their ulterior purpose. He had discerned a dangerous association of Gaelic, Catholic and radical political views, and was proceeding to take his counter-measures. The *Antiquities of Ireland* was the opening shot of a campaign.

During the next three decades the lines of division became quite clear. After 1800 Protestant and unionist antiquarians and historians worked, almost without exception, to undermine romantic or glorious conceptions of pre-Norman or pre-Danish Ireland, while their nationalist and Catholic counterparts strove to sustain and develop them. This polarisation had various interesting implications. We might draw attention again to the fact that Protestant denigration of the ancient Celtic culture was a new phenomenon. Before 1790 Irish Protestant scholarship had often seen in early Irish history purer and less adulterated social forms. We might note, for future reference, that this was to prove the case once more especially *after* 1870. Then, Anglo-Irish intellectuals, faced with an ebullient Home Rule (and, as they would generally have added, Rome Rule) movement, sought to trump it by playing the card of a Gaelic civilisation which predated the Christian bifurcation by a millenium or more. Again – to take another example of the curiosity of the affair – it is remarkable that although most of the historical protagonists of 1790– 1820 were in holy orders (of one sort or another) it was the character of pre-Christian Ireland which was being contested.

But what I especially wish to emphasise in the scholarly warfare over the resuscitated body of the Celtic past is the elision of time common to all the combatants. Time was being so foreshortened that the character of druidical Ireland was being treated as validating or invalidating, in some significant fashion, the early-nineteenth-century political and social order. In part, this use of antiquity as a touchstone of the present resembled the use made of the early Church by the religious reformers and counter-reformers in the theological disputations of the sixteenth century; but with the roles reversed. The nationalist–Catholic school saw the course of Irish history in terms of degeneration from an initial purity, whereas the unionist–Protestants presented it in terms of a triumphant, if lengthy and incomplete, emergence from barbarism.

A more directly political foreshortening of time rapidly succeeded the controversy on the sophistication of Celtic culture. The 1798 rebellion in Leinster was as stunning an event to contemporaries in Ireland as 1789 had been to French men and women in France. The floor of organised society had collapsed – albeit momentarily – and the established classes suddenly awoke to the existence of passions and hatred which they had hitherto relegated comfortably to a primeval phase in Britain's conquest of Ireland. In particular, the Ulster rising of 1641, when the Catholic survivors of the dispossessions of the previous generation had broken out without forewarning in revenge and counter-seizure, became the subject of intense historical exploration.

The essential question for Irish Protestants, at the very close of the eighteenth century, was whether 1641 had been misread by a foolishly generous posterity. Had it really indicated, unperceived, an ineradicable disposition towards savage retribution among the Catholic inhabitants of Ireland? This issue was made to bear directly upon the day-to-day politics of Ireland at the end of the 1790s.

The greatest matter for decision in that decade had been Catholic liberation from the penal code which had been designed to reduce the majority of the Irish population to what O'Connell was to call a helot state, and to keep them in that condition, by denying them access to arms, property and independent education, and to land, the guilds, the great professions, Parliament, government and local office. The 'treachery' and 'massacre' of 1641 had certainly been uppermost in the minds of those who had composed the penal code at the beginning of the eighteenth century. Servile masses without the possibility of servile war had been the object of that complex of deprivations and controls. But eighty years of comparative tranquillity, and the steady rationalisation of the religions in between, had softened the Anglo-Irish image of themselves as planted amongst savage and implacably hostile natives; and most of the repressive system had either fallen into desuetude or been dismantled by 1793.

The rationale of this benign modification in the Anglo-Irish outlook – although rarely expressed in explicit terms – was a developmental view of history. The process of enlightenment was supposed to have destroyed the possibility that men would any longer kill each other for religious reasons. The gradual economic, educational and social concessions to the moneyed Catholics, in fact if not in law, were supposed to have destroyed their more solid grievances by the 1780s. Nor was all this mere fancy on the part of the Protestant Ascendancy, even if the 'concessions' did look very different when viewed by the recipients instead of the conceders. Relatively speaking, the two middle quarters of the eighteenth century were remarkable for the degree of practical toleration of each other by the sects in Ireland. They were also marked by an increasing stream of prudential conversions from Catholicism to the Church of Ireland. In turn, these conversions reinforced the feeling that a new age was unfolding. Patently, many had conformed in order to hold or gain land or to practise law; and this surely implied that religion was no longer a passionate or even a serious concern. In these confident circumstances, it had been easy to relegate 1641 and the like to the shelf of 'old, unhappy far-off things'. Even Ulster Presbyterians tended to dissociate the present from the distant age of dark passions and bestial ferocity. It is true, as we shall see, that some of the very fruits of security and toleration, in particular the Catholic challenge to the near-exclusive Protestant ownership of land, at various social levels, gradually revived Protestant apprehensions. But down to the last few years of the eighteenth century, this amounted to little more than a vague, if general, unease.

The first premonitory shocks had come in the late 1780s. At one end of the system of Protestant Ascendancy, an attempt in 1787 by the Chief Secretary of the day, Thomas Orde, to deprive the Church of Ireland of its monopoly of primary and secondary education, and to take the first steps in 'un-denominationalising' Irish schools, aroused bitter Anglican opposition. Orde's scheme was denounced in the Irish House of Commons, in tones worthy of early Victorian evangelicalism, as the 'most fatal blow to the protestant religion in Ireland . . . nothing would be more grateful to the society *de propaganda fide* in Rome'.[2] At the other end of the social scale, the 'land war', which had since 1760 accompanied the rise in population and the contraction of the area of arable land in favour of pastoral husbandry, turned into sectarian conflict as it reached the border counties. In particular, the struggle for land was transmuted into a supremacist battle in those areas of Tyrone, Fermanagh and especially Armagh, where Catholics and Presbyterians were nearly equal in both numbers and degrees of poverty. The onset of the French Revolution in 1789 checked this deterioration for the moment. But the very cause of the arrest, further concessions to the Catholics under British governmental pressure, deepened Protestant fears; and these in turn produced a weakening in the British resolve and ultimately a volte-face in British policy. From 1793 onwards Ireland, despite some contrary appearances, was whirled about once more in a descending spiral of religious mistrust and dread.

But it was the Leinster rising of 1798 which really produced immediate, full and widespread reversions to seventeenth-century casts of mind. The relationship of that rising to the outbreak of 1641 became at once a critical matter for debate in Ireland. For the next ten years the problem of the 1640s engrossed the attention of Irish historians. Narratives by Musgrave, Duigenan and others in the Protestant school presented popery as the essential cause of the Leinster rebellion. Catholic fanaticism, they argued, had been the progenitor of every native uprising since the reformation. 'Popish bigotry' had caused the massacre of 1798, and that in precisely the same degree and fashion as it had caused the massacre of 1641. Their Catholic opponents reversed the entire affair. Taaffe, for example, argued in 1801 that in seventeenth-century Ireland (unlike seventeenth-century England) rebellion had been *in support* of monarchy. Two years later Plowden, another Catholic historian, wrote that the responsibility for 1641 rested squarely upon the English administration in Ireland, whose systematic persecution of the Catholics provoked the massacres: official cruelty, not popish bigotry, explained the horrors of the 1640s and the 1790s alike. In 1808 the counter-attack was fully developed in Cox's account of mid-seventeenth-century atrocities in which only those attributable to the Irish Protestants were examined.

After 1808, as the petitionary and pacific campaign for Catholic Emancipation revived under O'Connell's rising star, a new historical topic, the Treaty of Limerick of 1691, began to rise in prominence. It was soon to dominate Irish history writing as decisively as the massacre of 1641 had dominated it in the preceding years. Characteristically, in the light of the new Catholic leadership, the terms in which this latest conflict was cast were legal and constitutional. The critical points at issue were, first, the nature and meaning of William III's agreement with the French Crown in 1691 to grant religious toleration to the Irish Catholics; and secondly, the extent of the royal prerogative. Broadly speaking, Catholic–nationalist historians found that the Treaty of Limerick both constituted 'written civil law and translated their natural rights into a concrete reality, and no subsequent act of parliament could alter that fact'.[3] If there was some piquancy in the Catholic scholars' deploying natural rights theories, reinforced by concepts of fundamental law, there was still more in the Protestant–unionist (or Tory) historical school being driven to argue a utilitarian and anti-monarchical case, and to search for evidence to support a Whiggish view of 1688.

In turn, by the middle 1820s, the 1798 rising began to appear in nationalist historiography in its own right, paraded as the latest chapter of an age-old but unvarying struggle against English oppression. Characteristic of the new mood, tone and subject matter was the observation, in 1825, of Thomas McNeven, one of the earliest historians of the Leinster rising, that 'the present recollection of past events, if properly applied, would emancipate the catholics, or, better still, emancipate the Irish'.[4] Simultaneously, the concept of a golden *Christian* age which invasion from Britain had abruptly ended was taking shape and finding voice. As O'Connell expressed it in 1827:

Accursed be the day . . . when the invaders first touched our shores. They came to a nation famous for its love of learning, its piety, its heroism [and] . . . doomed Ireland to seven centuries of oppression.[5]

Two years later, in a private letter, O'Connell stressed the spiritual facet of this particular vision of the past more heavily:

Ireland seems to me to be the most proper nursery for spiritual needs – Irish priests are *in demand* all over the Christian world and in my day dreams I revive the brighter period of Irish history where Erin was the cradle of saints and science.[6]

Each of these developments of the 1820s was met antiphonally by a Protestant–unionist counterview. Each was also in itself portentous. For the two myths of repetitive heroic violence and of an early Christian Elysium of saints and scholars were to form staples of Irish nationalist culture for the next century or more. *Pari passu*, they reinforced a national feeling for the timeless. For 1798 was presented from the outset as but the latest item in an essentially undifferentiated series, while the age of spiritual empire was seen as merely overlaid by seven hundred years of English domination, ready to spring back in its original glory once the terrible weight of suppression had been removed.

III

In one sense, of course, the successive and overlapping historical debates of the late eighteenth and early nineteenth centuries in Ireland were ahistorical. It would be difficult to deny that all of them were politics by other means, although it is also true that somewhere amidst the heat and dust the foundations of modern historical scholarship in Ireland were being laid. But if change is the 'objective' historian's point of concern, time is the coinage in which he deals; and if this early phase of history-writing is remarkable for its imperception of change, it is no less remarkable for its concept of time. This is relevant to us today because the early history-writing both shaped and solidified what was to prove an enduring characteristic in Irish political attitudes. Negatively, it may be described as an absence of a developmental or sequential view of past events. Positively, it implies a mode or habit of judgement and apprehension outside a chronologically calibrated, or indeed any, time scale. It may be no coincidence that the society in which this mode or habit prevailed was deeply Christian. Ranke's celebrated phrase, 'Every generation is equidistant from eternity', was doubtless meant as a corrective to the Whig interpretation of history, that which follows the furrow of progress to the present and praises the dead ploughman who deviated least from the appointed line. But the phrase can also be usefully appropriated by the Christian – at any rate, by those Christians who sheer off from the idea of predestination. However dimly it may be perceived, however brokenly it may be expressed, the collision between God's foreknowledge of events and human choice is a matter of profound concern to them; and precisely the same applies to their obvious route of escape from this dilemma – the Christian view of God as standing outside time entirely, without yesterdays or tomorrows, omnipresent in an ever-present.

Such a view appears to me to approximate to the concept of the past which infused Irish historiography at its modern commencement and which still infuses the historical assumptions of most ordinary Irish people. Of course, this rendered and renders the past an arsenal of weapons with which to defend both inveterate prejudice and that ignorance which wishes only to remain invincible. But it also implies historical interpretations in terms of law and morals. In such a view, no statute of limitations softens the judgement to be made upon past events, however distant. In such a view, no prescriptive rights can be established by the passage of time, however lengthy.

The historical debate upon the Treaty of Limerick – like the debate, half-a-century later, upon the validity of the Act of Union of 1801 or the debate, another half-a-century on, upon the validity of the Anglo-Irish agreement of 1921 – provides a clear illustration of this mode of thought. In each case, it was concluded by many – and this was to serve as the determinant of their future conduct – that the proceeding itself was illegitimate. Let us apply such reasoning to our three instances in turn. In the first case, 1691, a solemn international engagement by the supreme executive authority in the land (such an argument ran) cannot be unilaterally repudiated by any, let alone an inferior, authority. In the second case, 1801, an undertaking between two Parliaments (the argument would run) cannot be binding where one had bribed and intimidated the other's members until a sufficient number of them acquiesced. In the third, 1921, the delegates bound by instructions to seek endorsement from a Cabinet before committing their signatures to a treaty (it would be said) commit nothing but themselves to charges of treachery if they sign of their own discretion. Thus the Catholic disabilities of the eighteenth century, the Union of 1801 and the Treaty of 1922 were or are, in the eyes of the incorruptibles of the 1820s, 1900s and 1980s respectively, legally null. It might, or may, be impracticable to behave as if the law were a nullity. It might, or may, be prudential to obey under protest and duress. But this in no way affected or affects the fundamental historical – which is also to say, the fundamental moral – reality. Moreover, prudence and policy were but matters of the hour, always liable to change. Thus, when, for example, Arthur Griffith called in 1905 for the establishment of an independent Irish assembly, and justified it, partly upon the ground that the Act of Union was 'a usurpation and a fraud', the mere fact that the United Kingdom Parliament had, for all practical purposes, exercised sovereignty over Ireland for more than a century was not regarded for one moment as a counter-balancing consideration. As the opening resolution of the Sinn Fein meeting of 1905 had it, 'the people of Ireland are a free people, and . . . no law made without their authority and consent is or can ever be binding on their conscience'.[7]

This sense of timeless justice spreads in all directions in Ireland, north as well as south, to fundamental law as well as natural right. On the one hand, as we have seen, the Treaty of Limerick was assumed by some to

stand as much because it expressed unalterable natural law as because it
had immutable constitutionality upon its side. Conversely Sir Edward
Carson, in opposing Home Rule for Ireland in the House of Commons in
1914, relied equally upon what he called the final legal establishment of
'civil and religious liberty' in 1689, and upon the argument that 'If these
[Ulster] men are not morally justified [in armed resistance] when they are
. . . driven out of one government with which they are satisfied and put
under another which they loathe, I do not see how resistance can ever be
justified in history'.[8] Similarly, in the Solemn League and Covenant of
1912 – the very name or notion of a 'Solemn League and Covenant' is of
course redolent of the seventeenth century – 'the men of Ulster', as the
signatories described themselves, 'humbly' relied 'on the God whom our
fathers in days of stress and trial [1689] confidently trusted'.[9] Similarly
with the other Irish Protestants, although their fixed point was the
eighteenth- rather than the seventeenth-century experience. Taking up
Bishop Berkeley's phrase, 'We Irish', of two centuries before, Yeats
spoke in 1933 for the Anglo-Irish of the south in equivalent terms:

> We Irish, born into that ancient sect
> But thrown upon this filthy modern tide
> And by its formless spawning fury wrecked,
> Climb to our proper dark, that we may trace
> The lineaments of a plummet-measured face.

But timelessness might also have a most practical and literal meaning
for those looking back upon the Irish past. Let me take as one example
O'Connell's reflections of 1828 upon his failure to secure Catholic
Emancipation three years before, despite his concession to the British
government of the two so-called 'wings' or securities – one, state payment of the Catholic clergy, and the other, the disenfranchisement of the
almost exclusively Catholic 40s freehold voters. Because he was determining parliamentary strategy on the eve of its first application by Irish
nationalists in the House of Commons, O'Connell's reading of history
may well have been a fateful one, casting shadows ahead for the subsequent ninety years. 'In fact', O'Connell wrote, shortly before the famous
Clare election of 1828,

> we were carrying the Emancipation bill [in 1825] not by reason of the
> political wisdom of the Ministry but from the apprehension [it] enter-
> tained of the resentment of the Irish nation. . . . The course I should
> have taken was to have kept up that salutary apprehension and I could
> easily have done so but, instead of that I listened in an evil hour to the
> suggestion of Mr. Plunket, etc., who said that if we conceded 'the
> Wings' by way of security, we should certainly carry the bill . . . I
> procured for this purpose public tranquillity. The Ministry saw that I
> had appeased the storm, they considered that the danger was passed

and the House of Lords scouted our Emancipation bill. Nay, Peel . . .
actually taunted me with having betrayed popular rights in order to
attain the objects of my personal ambition. I was deceived once but I
should indeed be . . . 'a knave or a fool' if [I] were to be deceived . . .
again. We shall never be emancipated but as we were relieved in 1778,
1782 and 1793, that is, when it becomes necessary for the English
Government to do something for Ireland.[10]

O'Connell is presenting here a pragmatic or experiential, rather than a
moral or legal, historical judgement. But in the essential matter of the
time-frame, he is at one with the other strand in Irish historical thought.
He assumes an absolute repetitive form to lie at the heart of Anglo-Irish
dealings. Whether it is 1778, 1782, 1793 or 1825 the same forces operate
in the same fashion. There is a constant relationship between the oscillation of coercion and conciliation on the part of the overlord and the
oscillation of negotiation and the threat of violence upon the part of the
subjected. *Mutatis mutandis*, Butt, Parnell and Redmond, or for that
matter O'Neill, Faulkner and John Hume in Northern Ireland in recent
years, have analysed their various predicaments in substantially the same
terms and with substantially the same assumptions about the repetitive-
ness of the historical process.

IV

In *Viewless Winds* a Sydney surgeon, Herbert Moran, describes the
reactions of his father, an Irish-Australian, to the Civil War in Ireland
when he returned to his homeland for the last time in 1922:

For him this was the final stage of his disillusionment. He could not
understand it. So back he turned gladly to Australia. Between him and
Ireland there was now more than a world of miles. There were centuries, aeons, the span of a man's struggle and triumph in a new land.[11]

We may take this peculiarly dramatic conversion from one temporal
framework to its opposite as a text for the consideration of the British
counterpart of what we have been discussing. As the concept of the
contemporiety of the past came to dominate popular historical thought in
Ireland in the late eighteenth and early nineteenth century, a counter-
concept of history, that of beneficial development, was gradually
triumphing in Britain. It was fitting that congratulatory history should
have come to predominate there through the work of the master-
celebrator, Macaulay. Let me attempt, by way of the single example of
the master, to indicate certain of the characteristics of this chronological
outlook.

First, Macaulay's iron faith in progress embraced the moral as well as the material. Faced with the discovery of double-dealing by his seventeenth-century hero, Sidney, he found it

> some consolation to reflect that in our time, a public man would be lost to all sense of duty and of shame, who would not spurn from him a temptation which conquered the virtue and the pride of Algernon Sydney.[12]

But the moral and the material were ultimately commingled in the grand advance. Complacently, Macaulay described the supersession, from one century to the next, of 'the savage tragedy of the Argyll rebellion' by the commercial prosperity of modern Greenock; and this 'was, of course, pointing a moral by contrast, fulfilling the pledge at the opening of the *History* to refute those who sighed for a past superior to the present'.[13] Nor did he reserve his strenuous optimism for his books. His tergiversations and rationalisations on the contemporary issue of child employment neatly illustrate its uses in his own conduct. Between 1830 and 1845 Macaulay had been a leading opponent of factory reform in the interests of children and women. But in 1847 he, like many other Liberal members of the House of Commons, changed his mind. Characteristically, he then struck the note of progress which the mass of his educated compatriots wished to hear:

> the practice of setting children prematurely to work, a practice which the state, the legitimate protector of those who cannot protect themselves, has, in our time, wisely and humanely interdicted, prevailed in the seventeenth century to an extent which, when compared to the extent of the manufacturing system, seems almost incredible. . . . The more carefully we examine the history of the past, the more reason shall we find to dissent from those who imagine that our age has been fruitful of new social evils. The truth is that the evils are, with scarcely an exception, old. That which is new is the intelligence which discerns and the humanity which remedies them.[14]

Here was a view of time in which past evils were weighted according to the lesser potentiality for evil which existed in simpler circumstances. Here was a view of time in which the march of reason, of knowledge and of compassion was steadily diminishing the relative power and extent of immorality. All the judgements and estimates were, so to speak, calibrated for amelioration on a measure marked off by half-centuries or even decades; and, in such a framework, a sudden turnabout in attitude, such as his own on the factory question, might be a matter not for apology but for satisfaction. The corollary of such moral expansionism was a corresponding diminution of any sense of responsibility for the past. It even declined steadily in significance as it receded.

High Whig history has not of course survived in England – at any rate, not wholly or in its first crude colours. But the two truly essential elements of its conception of time, relativism and steadily declining responsibility for, and interest in, the receding past, have outlived the death of Macaulayism in the general historical thinking of its birthplace. Complacency about the present and abounding faith in the future may have disappeared; but these were mere ornamental features of this cast of mind. The cast itself could and did, and perhaps still does, endure in England, long after their disappearance.

I do not mean, of course, to suggest that the respective common historical assumptions of the two peoples were, or are, either innate or universal. As we have seen, mid-eighteenth-century Ireland was conventionally 'enlightened' in its view of the earlier past. Conversely, there were bodies in Victorian England whose historical view was timeless and moral, at least upon religious subjects: the fires of Smithfield and the braziers on the Devon headlands burned as if it were yesterday in the imaginations of millions of Evangelicals. None the less the contrast stood and stands as generally valid. In terms of norms and masses, it *is* true that the Irish do not forget and that the English do not remember.

Given these crosspurposes of historical thought and impressions, one of the leading tasks in almost any Anglo-Irish analysis – and not least the analysis of the imbroglio of the last decade and a half – is to search out and fix the different sets of assumptions and the different meanings attached to words and symbols by the generality of people in each tradition. The failure of mutual comprehension has sometimes been very plain, and the consequences have often been of first importance. Take, as an instance of both together, John Redmond's speech as leader of the Irish Nationalist Party, to the House of Commons on 3 August 1914, as war with the German empire was almost upon them:

> The House will remember that in 1778, at the end of the disastrous American War, when . . . the military power of this country was almost at its lowest ebb, and when the shores of Ireland were threatened with foreign invasion, a body of 100,000 Irish Volunteers sprang into existence for the purpose of defending her shores . . . from the very first day, the Catholics of the South and West subscribed money and sent it toward the arming of their Protestant fellow-countrymen . . . in the North. May history repeat itself to-day? There are in Ireland two large bodies of Volunteers [the Ulster Volunteer Force (UVF) and National Volunteers] . . . I say to the [British] Government that they may tomorrow withdraw every one of their troops from Ireland. I say that the coast of Ireland will be defended from foreign invasion by her armed sons, and for this purpose armed Nationalist

Catholics in the South will be only too glad to join arms with the armed Protestant Ulstermen in the North . . .[15]

Redmond's meaning, to all Irish auditors, whether they heard him with horror or delight, was that 'Grattan's Parliament' should be reinaugurated in the same fashion and by the same means as in 1782, and that sectarian conflict in Ireland should be overridden in the same fashion as the Patriot movement of the 1780s was supposed at the time to have overridden the religious polarisation obtaining there since 1691. But to British auditors, Redmond's speech simply signified Irish support for the imminent war effort. Doubtless a whiff or two of patriotic–sentimental rodomontade were necessary for him to draw quietly the surviving stumps of any dragon's teeth which their ancestors might inadvertently have sown. But what a bagatelle was this in the general state of things! The consequences of the gross, almost comic, divergence in interpretation cannot be calculated exactly. But it seems to me quite an arguable proposition that without its occurrence and the subsequent crosspurposes, the Easter Rising of 1916 might have proved impossible to mount.

For a modern counterpart, in the current Irish crisis, the official decision to permit the Apprentice Boys' march in Derry in August 1969 may perhaps serve as an example. The Irish connotation of the march was the annual reassertion of the power relationships and arrangement of rank and station stamped in 1689 upon a certain territory. The British view, however – these were early days – was that of the district commissioner called on to allow or disallow a tribal ritual. The decision was Britain's, but the immediate consequences were Northern Ireland's. To paraphrase T. P. O'Connor's famous phrase of ninety years before, it was another demonstration of the consequences of attempting to govern one country through the popular – indeed, the vulgar – conceptions of another.

But it is not solely a matter of the British mishearing of Irish voices, and British mistakes in decoding Irish messages. The misunderstandings do not all cluster on one side of St George's Channel, and the Irish Sea. I have had an eye to the decisions consequent on this sort of error, and normally, over the past two centuries, decisions of such a kind have been London's business. But if we notice, for example, among comparatively recent happenings, the conviction of SAS men for bearing arms in the Republic, or the pressing of charges of torturing against the United Kingdom in the Court of Human Rights, we can see the same forces in operation in the other capital, the capital of the Republic. Britain is engrossed with an immediate problem. She assumes a common war effort because there is a common general interest. She sees herself as a state quite remarkable for its ready forgiveness of transgressions, and *therefore* entitled to ready pardon. But these are not pleas which can be heard clearly by Irish ears. They are drowned or distorted by the noises of the old coercion, old condescension, old colonialism and old battles for parity and the rule of ordinary law.

The cases touched on have been all large and open instances of misinterpretation of political language, and of failure to comprehend the temporal and historical frame of reference being employed. But such cases, and they could readily be multiplied, are merely peaks in a mountain range; and they rise moreover from a scarcely perceptible, yet boundless, plateau of everyday ambiguity. Cumulatively, it is perhaps a mass of commonplace, unnoticed discordance of meaning and connotation which has set and still sets Anglo-Irish communication most askew.

Finally, the characteristic Irish time-frame has coloured Irish political prediction and, through this means also, has affected present practice. Moral, legal and experiential views of history induce a cyclical view as well. Of course, cyclicalists can originate elsewhere; otherwise whence Machiavelli or Vico? But a past seen in terms of subjection and struggle, seen as a pageant or tournament of heroic defeat, is one of the roads towards a fundamental distrust of or even disbelief in achievement. Again, this is not an exclusive derivation. Splendid failure can work quite differently in national myth; otherwise, what price, in the Australian experience, Eureka or Gallipoli? None the less is it true that the characteristic Irish time-frame inclines Irishmen to a repetitive view of history and that such a view inclines them – perhaps in defensive wariness and from fear of failure – to prize the moral as against the actual, and the bearing of witness as against success. The *locus classicus* of this cast of mind is the Proclamation of the Republic on Easter Monday 1916. Six times, it said, in the preceding three centuries had the fact of Ireland's independence been asserted by force of arms. The honour of the current generation was being vindicated by a seventh heroic assertion by force of arms. As Chesterton later observed, the signatories spoke not so much of success as of bearing witness: 'They desired to be [martyrs] in the Greek and literal sense.' [16] The other side of the coin of historical pessimism is the hollowness of the heroic stance and the degeneration of the noble action. Yeats faithfully reflected this second face of Irish cyclicalism in 1921:

> The night can sweat with terror as before
> We pieced our thoughts into philosophy,
> And planned to bring the world under a rule,
> Who are but weasels fighting in a hole.
> . . .
> We, who seven years ago
> Talked of honour and of truth,
> Shriek with pleasure if we show
> The weasel's twist, the weasel's tooth.

Almost a century earlier, Mangan had conveyed still more strikingly the national sense of the illusoriness of apparent achievement and the suddenness with which fair prospects might dissolve. The final stanzas of his *Vision of Connacht in the Thirteenth Century* describe the ending of the feast:

> . . . behold! – a change
> From light to darkness, from joy to woe!
> King, nobles, all,
> Looked aghast and strange;
> The minstrel-group sate in dumbest show!
> Had some great crime
> Wrought this dread amaze,
> This terror? None seemed to understand . . .
> I again walked forth;
> But lo! the sky
> Showed fleckt with blood, and an alien sun
> Glared from the north,
> And there stood on high,
> Amid his short beams, a skeleton!

But what of those other Irishmen, the northern Protestants, whose corporate principle of being rests upon the success of the Boyne in 1690? Are they truly different from the remainder? The siege of Derry of 1689 is their original and most powerful myth. They see themselves in that, and since then, as an embattled and enduring people. Their historical self-vision is one of an endless repetition of repelled assaults, without hope of absolute finality or of fundamental change in their relationship to their surrounding and surrounded neighbours. In the last analysis they share the historical cyclicalism of nationalist Ireland, or at least the two mental habits tend to converge. The one may take shape as insurgent and degenerative successively, the other as beleaguerment. But their rhythms, their ultimate world-views, are extraordinarily similar. This being so, such a phrase as 'the solution' or 'a solution' to the Northern Ireland question has little meaning or promise for either. They are committed too deeply to ancient roles and modes of interpreting the historical flow, and the patterns they perceive in – or, if you will, impose upon – the past, are at once a cause of the present crisis, and a force making for its continuance. Each would add, of course, that the present crisis is also an effect of many past crises which conformed to and which in retrospect constitute the fatal pattern.

Chapter 2

Place

I

In one sense, the Irish problem has persisted because of the power of geographical images over men's minds. In particular, the image of the island, with the surrounding water carving out a territorial identity, has been compelling. This is not strange. From its Homeric beginnings, European literature has been infused by this physical–geographical symbol of separateness, mystery and peculiarity. Nor, in the case of Ireland at least, is the image powerful only among the oldest or the most numerous body of the inhabitants. The Protestant Nation of the late eighteenth century was self-consciously *arriviste* and small in numbers. Yet it proudly and confidently asserted its identity; and this identity derived from the sea-made isolation. When the Act of Union between Great Britain and Ireland was being mooted, the Irish Bar almost *en bloc* resisted – all else apart, they believed that it would cost them much of their business and standing. At their final meeting of protest in 1799 Goold, a leading counsel, drew the loudest cheers with this particular passage:

> there are 40,000 British troops in Ireland, [yet] with 40,000 bayonets at my breast the minister shall not plant another Sicily in the bosom of the Atlantic. Our patent to be a state, not a shire, came direct from Heaven. The Almighty has, in majestic characters, signed the great charter of our independence. The great Creator of the world has given our beloved country the gigantic outlines of a kingdom. The God of nature never intended that Ireland should be a province, and by God she never shall.[1]

In some respects there was nothing new about such a declaration as Goold's. The invaders of seven centuries had had, in the nature of things, to define themselves somehow; and the obvious course was to do so in terms of their distance and physical separation from the mainland. Moreover, formally distinct Parliaments and structures of law and administration – above all the formal distinction between the kingdoms of Ireland and England or Great Britain – had always represented the island as an entity. The sixteenth century had destroyed even all interior qualifications upon such a concept. The Pale had then disappeared. So also had its opposite, the large tract of country in mid- and west Ulster, which had been practically immune in the Elizabethan years to even partial colonisation. Gone too was the species of apartheid embodied in such a code as the Statutes of Kilkenny. In the minds of the planters of the Williamite era, Ireland was as undifferentiated internally, part by part, as it was differentiated externally by its formal constitution and still more by its abasing, newly reproven colonyhood.

Colonyhood was however a negative sort of entity. The area concerned might have been limned by God in water, but its character had been determined by England. It was the absence of English powers and rights which, in the eyes of the settlers, marked off their portion of the British Isles from the remainder. They could not but see that the 'dual monarchy' was a pretence, their Parliament an empty show and even the appurtenances of law and social control derivative. These were the fruits of the Whig Settlement of 1689–91. Yet ironically it was the rise of native Whiggery in the dependency which was to turn Irish insularity inside out in terms of political imagery and implication.

Wolfe Tone once confessed that his 'great discovery' – that 'the influence of England was the radical vice of our Government'[2] – was to be found in the writings of Molyneaux and Swift. He meant that Molyneaux and Swift had provided very early (though not the very first) expressions of the resentment and injured *amour propre* bred by the colonial condition. This was true although it was also the case that the initial opposition to the metropolis was halting and limited. The sense of grievance developed slowly in the eighteenth century; and it was always muted by the fear of dispossession should England's support ever weaken. It also manifested itself as a mere demand for the individual rights and constitutional arrangements which the counterparts of the Ascendancy enjoyed in England. In short the discontent was that of transplanted *Englishmen* suffering in *England's* service. None the less a critical change in direction had been made. The Irish entity was being redefined as a deprived and spoliated as well as a dependent country.

Moreover, as the eighteenth century wore on Ireland became increasingly homogeneous, politically and administratively speaking. The reason was simple. The Anglo-Irish Ascendancy was a thinly scattered ruling caste. Of course, their density varied considerably from region to region. But everywhere they were comparatively sparse in numbers. This meant that regional or shire government, and county society after the English pattern, were impossible. Curiously, though not surprisingly, the fewness in numbers induced a national rather than a local outlook, and also concerted action. What was shire business in England and Wales was often national business in Ireland; and the solidarity of the Irish ruling class transcended county and provincial loyalties. These characteristics became still more marked in the second half of the century, and especially after 1760, as internal communications improved and parliamentary sessions became more and more frequent, as well as longer in duration. Thus, paradoxically, the relative poverty and paucity of numbers of the Irish Ascendancy rendered Dublin a capital to a degree beyond that of even London, and College Green a power-club to a degree beyond that of even Westminster.

In this fashion, the ground was laid for the emergence of the idea of a Nation conterminous with the Irish island. To the legal fiction of an independent Irish kingdom was added the resentments of the Irish planters and the centrifugal pressures of their small numbers and meagre circumstances. Initially this Nation emerged as 'Protestant'. The term was however misleading. It did not embrace, at first, the Irish Presbyterians and other Nonconformists or even the poorer or unpropertied members of the Church of Ireland. 'Protestant', in this context, indicated and emphasised the traditional anti-popery and self-defensive anti-Jacobitism of the Irish aristocracy, gentry, clergymen and lawyers. But however few its members and for whatever ends they strove, the 'Irish Nation' had from its beginnings *faute de mieux* to define Irish nationality in terms of Irish residence or birth. This was critically important.

The last quarter of the eighteenth century saw some curious exits and entrances in this affair. In general, by 1800 the Irish Nation had been vacated by its initial occupiers. The Ascendancy as a whole had moved back to its old condition of conscious – not to add, abject – dependency upon Great Britain. They had become again outer Britons. The richest indeed often became inner Britons as well by permanent settlement or seasonal migration, and by choosing English places of education for their sons. And even among the rest the steadily growing practice of military or imperial service drew them away from an essentially Irish identification. The Irish Anglican bourgeoisie and tradesmen, who had followed the Ascendancy into the Irish Nation in the late 1770s and 1780s, by and large followed them out. The case of the Ulster Presbyterians was the most interesting of all. Their experience of Irish Nationhood was at once more intense and shorter-lived than any other. The final decade of the eighteenth century saw both an Ulster domination of the national idea – with revolutionary, separatist and even republican overtones – and an Ulster reversion to an obsessive anti-popery which seemed to require a full-blooded British allegiance for security.

Thus by 1800 considerable numbers of all the Protestant groups had passed into and out of the Irish Nation with extraordinary rapidity. By default it had fallen into the hands of its latest entrants, the politicised Irish Catholic middle class. In a sense indeed it was their admission, or forcible entry, which had precipitated the departure of the rest. At any rate, it was rising Catholic pressure for civil equality which had launched the train of events that ended in the rising of 1798, and it was this Leinster rebellion which precipitated the final Protestant exodus. The next two generations were to see the process completed. Between 1795

and 1845 the mass of the Catholic peasantry were indoctrinated in the
concept of Irish Nationhood which became increasingly identified with
their particular culture and religion.

Yet both the Ascendancy origin and the short-lived Protestant possession of the idea of the Irish Nation proved to be of lasting significance.
The first ensured that the idea would be conceived of in terms of the
entire island, no more no less. It also ensured the domination of the
administrative and political capital, Dublin, within this entity. Irish
government may have been only formally autonomous *vis-à-vis* Westminster, but it was genuinely – in fact, by contemporary European
standards, extraordinarily – national *vis-à-vis* the interior and the
regions. Secondly, the initial Protestant possession of the idea of the
Nation, and in particular the brief phase in which it was dominated by
the northern dissenters, had rendered it non-sectarian – at least in the
ideal. In other words, the Irish Nation was now stamped with the
assertions that Irish domicile *per se* created Irish nationality, and that this
nationality dwarfed religious no less than any other differences between
Irishmen. Since these dogmas flew in the face of facts – in particular,
the facts that many Irish Protestants classified themselves primarily as
British, and that most Irish Protestants regarded religious and not secular allegiance as the primary principle of division in society – some
further justification was imperative. Hence the theory of the 'false
unconsciousness' of Protestants. That they belonged to the Irish Nation
without knowing it required some explanation. It was found in the
connection with England. It was in England's interest to bribe and
confuse a sufficient minority of Irishmen to control the island politically.
A collaborationist class was, as usual, a prerequisite of domination: the
imperial power lacked the manpower and resources to rule by naked,
imported force. Religion, land and office, but chiefly the first, were the
means by which Britain produced the fatal distinctions and conflicts
among Irishmen: by these, she divided and ruled. Thus Irish nationalism
through its eighteenth-century Protestant origins came to acquire two of
its leading articles of faith: Ireland's geographical integrity and Ireland's
irrefragable unity as a society. A third developed as a species of gloss
upon the first and second: this was that Britain ruled by fomenting
artificial discord.

II

From all this sprang the respective neuroses concerning place which
afflicted the different Irish sections in the nineteenth and twentieth
centuries. The first of these, in terms of current interest if not of time,
was the development of a sense of separateness among northern Protestants. The Ulster Protestant sense of territoriality manifested itself

remarkably clearly and early in the history of Ireland under the Union. Equally striking was their opponents' recognition – even if it was, presumably, accompanied by a tacit repudiation – of this claim to local supremacy. The explanation is simple. It was the rise of Catholic power in Ireland which led to the specification and articulation of Ulster 'separateness'. Its first public manifestation can be located precisely. It was an indirect consequence of O'Connell's success at the Clare election in July 1828. This had been dearly bought, financially speaking. Fresh Catholic rents poured in but not in sufficient volume to pay off the debt; and it was decided to tap a new source of money by organising the Catholics of northern Ireland, who had hitherto not been formed into cadres of the Catholic Association. The new exultant confidence bred of the Clare victory, and the desire to maintain the forward momentum of the movement by opening up a fresh area of action, were probably subsidiary motives in the decision.

It is instructive to look at the sequel through the eyes of a southern Catholic, Thomas Wyse, the historian as well as a leading member of the Association. Wyse regarded the attempt as little less than a 'direct provocative to open combat . . . Many of the most considerate [thoughtful] Ulster Catholics deprecated this unadvised *intrusion on the territory of their enemies*'.[3] John Lawless, the delegate who was to organise the north, hovered for weeks on the Ulster border, holding huge meetings at such nearby towns as Kells and Dundalk, and establishing branches of the Association, without hindrance, in the contiguous counties of Louth and Meath. In these counties the Protestant population was far from inconsiderable. But their identity as parts of Leinster seems to have provided a sort of immunity to Orange opposition. When however Lawless at last decided to cross the provincial border, the first considerable town in Co. Monaghan, Ballybay, was designated as the point of confrontation. Soon, thousands of armed Orangemen faced more thousands of armed Catholics from opposite hills overshadowing the town. At the eleventh hour, Lawless took fright, mounted a grey horse, rode through the ranks behind him – and fled. To the humiliation of the Catholics, the attempted 'invasion' was over.

How strange is all this on the face of things. The Catholic Association proclaimed itself to be a legal, sedulously peaceful, thoroughly established organisation for mutual advancement; and this could not fairly be gainsaid. The 'invaded' county, Monaghan, was not only overwhelmingly Catholic in population but also one of the four in which a revolt of the Catholic 40s freeholders in the general election of 1826 had broken landlord control of the constituency. Yet even Wyse, as we have seen, so far allowed the implicit claims of the northern Protestants as to speak of 'intrusion', border-crossing and 'provocation'. His account had continued in the martial and territorial strains:

The time now seemed arrived for the subjugation of the 'black North'.
Mr Lawless determined to enter it at Ballybay. . . . The Orangemen
were alarmed at the hostile incursion, and prepared for defence.[4]

Thus there can be no doubt that a set of county limits, quite unmarked
physically except on the pages of the map books, was accepted by foe as
well as friend as designating some sort of sovereignty. In defiance of
familiar and indisputable demographic, geographical and constitutional
fact, Ulster, an entity entirely lacking in even administrative significance
or religious or cultural homogeneity, was regarded as quite separate from
the rest of Ireland, and taken to be a Protestant preserve.

A still more striking demonstration of this assertion of and virtual
acquiescence in territoriality came with O'Connell's visit to Belfast in
1841. Early in that year, the Revd Dr Cooke, a fierce Orange divine,
challenged O'Connell to a public debate there on Repeal. O'Connell
replied, 'Dr Cooke, that odious theologue, was a fool in sending me this
challenge, and I should be another fool in accepting it.' [5] But the charges
of poltroonery which immediately followed this reply goaded him into
taking up half the gauntlet; and he accepted an invitation – possibly
prearranged – to address a Repeal Association meeting and dinner in
Belfast. At once, he was threatened on all sides with personal violence
should he enter Ulster. The border was to be 'guarded' and Orange
contingents mustered along the main road to Belfast at towns such as
Banbridge and Lisburn. The threats and placards calling for assemblies
of Protestant 'repellers' used one term above all other – 'invasion'. In the
event, O'Connell reached Belfast scathless by assuming an alias, travel-
ling two days before his appointed time and following obscure minor
roads. But the subterfuge only aggravated the Protestant obsession with
their preserve. Their country had been violated; and it was all too
characteristic of their enemies that this should have been achieved
cravenly and by craft.

The definitive formulation of Ulster identity under the threat of Home
Rule in 1886 was preceded by a similar fearful invasion. In 1883 the
Parnellite party attempted to win the Ulster constituency of Monaghan.
It is clear from William O'Brien's account that this was regarded as an
especially daring and dangerous venture. It was one thing to organise the
Catholic voters of the north to support a Liberal Protestant candidate.
But to run a Nationalist, and a Catholic at that, was seen by even its
proposers as an incursion. Yet how strange this was. Almost 75 per cent
of Monaghan's population was Catholic, and in the event T. M. Healy
outpolled the Conservative and Liberal candidates together in the by-
election. Indeed, thirty years later the majority of the Ulster constituencies (seventeen as against sixteen) were represented by Nationalist MPs,
most of them Catholics into the bargain. Thus, the hesitations, the
screwing-up of courage to the sticking-point, even at the century's end,

testified strikingly to the force of the Ulster image even among its enemies. They were soon to feel its force more powerfully.

The response of northern Protestants to first the rumours and then the reality of Gladstone's conversion to Home Rule was to organise an Ulster Unionist Party (UUP). This was of course officially opposed to the concession of Home Rule to any part of Ireland. But in reality it marked the beginning of Ulster separatism, as well as the abandonment of the traditional Liberal–Conservative and Anglican–Presbyterian conflicts in the north in face of the common peril. Although the new consensus was to be strained and threatened by various internal divisions among Ulster Protestants in the 'quiet' years, 1900–5, a northern Protestant community, or even *people*, had finally revealed itself to itself, and determined upon the entire province of Ulster as its territory.

It is true that at least until 1912 – and doubtless in many cases down to 1914 itself – other Irish and British Unionists regarded the Ulster resistance as a weapon against Home Rule in any form. It was widely assumed that Ireland was economically indivisible and that therefore Ulster's exemption from Home Rule would render the concession impracticable for the remainder of the island. But for the northerners themselves this was essentially a bonus. Their real purpose was to save themselves by saving their province, whatever the fate of the rest of Ireland. Under Carson's leadership, from 1911 onwards, the UUP was deployed against Home Rule in general: Carson himself either subscribed or pretended to subscribe to the extra-Ulster purposes to improve this bargaining power. The Covenant, the Volunteer Force and the projected Provisional Government, however, were all specifically Ulster phenomena, designed to cut Ulster off from the three other Irish provinces. Conversely any attempt to divide Ulster into its predominantly Protestant and predominantly Catholic parts was ferociously resisted. The Agar–Robartes proposal of 1912 to exempt the four 'plantation counties', Antrim, Armagh, Derry and Down, from the Home Rule Bill was scorned by the Ulster Unionists, although for immediate tactical reasons they voted in its favour. 'We do not accept this amendment as a compromise of the question,' declared Carson, 'No compromise is possible.'[6] Even later Liberal compromise suggestions which added two counties with small Catholic majorities, Fermanagh and Tyrone, to the list of the exempted, were at first angrily rejected.

By the time of the Buckingham Palace Conference of July 1914, however, there were signs that 'Ulster' might have to be redefined. Indeed, a prominent Ulster Unionist, Thomas Sinclair, had already redefined it with a bland subordination of topography to self-interest: 'By Ulster, I mean the six counties, Antrim, Down, Londonderry, Armagh, Tyrone, Fermanagh, with the important adjacent Unionist sections of Monaghan, Cavan and Donegal.'[7] Certainly, if counties, the basic units of provinces, were to be considered individually, three in

Ulster, Cavan, Donegal and Monaghan, were so overwhelmingly Catholic–Nationalist in composition that the case for their exemption from Home Rule was unsustainable, so long as numbers counted for anything at all. By the same token Ulster Unionists began to see them as a threat to maintaining a separate domain in the north-east. Border areas in which Protestants were outnumbered by three or four to one would be inherently destabilising. This is the background to the 'supreme sacrifice' of 1916 whereby the northern Unionists accepted the contraction of 'Ulster' to six counties.

Contracted Ulster certainly sacrificed the concept of the integral province. Yet it retained, in common usage, the word, and more important still the idea, of an inviolable territory. The refusal of the Northern Ireland government in 1922–3 to appoint a member to the Boundary Commission is testimony to this. But most important of all the image of the separate province had done much, perhaps everything, to determine the actual border which eventually divided Ireland politically. The province *per se* was maintained by northern Protestants as their objective till the eleventh hour; and when pressures and prudence alike enforced a contraction, the province still dominated their minds. For the withdrawal was cast in terms of its constituent units, the counties.

Why should the province or the county have been used at all in determining which portions of Ireland were to remain within the United Kingdom? The parliamentary constituencies were a much finer measure. Moreover, they spoke directly on the very point at issue when they returned Unionists or Nationalists at elections. Had this mode been adopted South Armagh, South Down and South Fermanagh and three-quarters of Tyrone would never have formed part of Northern Ireland. (After the boundary changes of 1918, half Fermanagh, half Down, two-thirds of Tyrone and perhaps the city of Derry and its western hinterland would have gone south.) This would have left West Belfast as the sole Catholic–Nationalist political stronghold behind the border.

Poor law unions formed another sort of electoral unit, more refined than counties; and doubtless a dividing line based on their representation would have given a similar though not identical result. Alternatively, a referendum based on polling districts was by no means impracticable even in 1914. Indeed, the Conservatives themselves pressed for one at that time, in the United Kingdom as a whole, on the very issue of Home Rule. As for the early 1920s, when the border was in fact determined, plebiscites were a then commonplace, the accepted European mode of determining a population's choice of allegiance. Thus, the Northern Ireland of 1921 and later years was in a real sense the product of geographical images, first that of a province, then that of a province less the least harmonious blocks of which it had been built – built, that is, in the administrative imagination. Had its extent been decided in any other likely fashion – above all, had the ordinary modes of decision of the twentieth century been adopted – its contours, and therefore its history, would have been quite another thing. Conversely as partition loomed larger on the horizon, some northern Protestants toyed with a different sort of political–geographical image, that of the cordon sanitaire. Fisher, the Northern Ireland representative on the Boundary Commission of 1923–5, actually advocated, in private, a considerable enlargement of the province's territory, to include Co. Donegal, more than 80 per cent Catholic in population. This would have reduced the border to be 'defended' by many miles. As for the recaptured Catholics, Fisher spoke of them as a sort of border tribe, using the analogy of Afghanistan and India and the imagery of 'the white man's burden'. Needless to add, Irish history would again have been changed profoundly had a cordon sanitaire revision of the notion of 'Ulster' carried the day.

III

It may well be wondered why Irish nationalists allowed a concept of place so unfavourable to themselves to dominate down to 5 December 1921, if not indeed later. The fundamental explanation lies in their own concept of place. Both the radical and the moderate wings of Irish nationalism, each overwhelmingly Catholic in composition from 1800 on, accepted the image of the Irish Nation as adumbrated first by the liberal wing of Anglo-Irish Ascendancy, and then developed in an inclusive, supra-sectarian direction by the dissenting and bourgeois 'left' among Irish Protestants. This meant blind assumptions that Ireland was one and indivisible politically, and that religion was a false divider of Irishmen, used as such by British governments intent on maintaining control of the island.

O'Connellism shared these assumptions fully with Toneism: the two differed radically on republicanism, on the desirable degree of separation from Great Britain and on the use of violence, but not on either the comprehensiveness or the secular character of the Irish Nation. O'Connell's adherence to these last principles was especially significant for it was he who gave shape and direction to the mass nationalism which he evoked in the second quarter of the nineteenth century. In the very first act of his political career, speaking at a public meeting of Catholics in Dublin in 1800 in protest against the Act of Union, he called on his audience to proclaim that even if the alternative to the Union were 'the re-enactment of the Penal Code in all its pristine horrors', they would still not hesitate to choose the latter as the more sufferable evil: 'that [they] would rather confide in the justice of the Protestants of Ireland than lay [their] country at the feet of foreigners'. When the meeting responded ecstatically, he continued, 'Yes, I know that the Catholics of Ireland still remember that they have a country, and that they would never accept any advantages as a sect that would destroy them as a people'.[8]

The antitheses 'Catholics' and 'country' and 'sect' and 'people' are of course significant. Eleven years later O'Connell repeated the substance of this speech in his still more celebrated address to the Repeal meeting of 1811, adding the accusation that Britain deliberately fomented religious divisions among Irishmen to blind them to the oneness of their nationality:

> the real cause of the Union lay deeper, but it is quite obvious. It is to be found at once in the religious dissensions which the enemies of Ireland have created and continued . . . separating us into wretched sections and miserable sub-divisions.[9]

Thus the essential political unity and distinctness of the island, the secondary importance of its sectarian groupings and the use of religious bigotry and fear by Great Britain to control the entire dependency became articles of faith for constitutional no less than revolutionary nationalism. O'Connell maintained and indoctrinated his followers in these dogmas until his last days, and they were transmitted intact to the parliamentary parties of later generations. So indeed was 'place' in a much more particular and exact sense. O'Connell had attended debates in the Irish Parliament at College Green, and in 1797 daydreamed about his own performances there in later years. The very building became for him a symbol of what was to be restituted; and this too passed down to Parnellism. Throughout the nineteenth century the Bank of Ireland, in the heart of Dublin, remained unchanged externally from the days when it had accommodated the Irish Houses of Lords and Commons. As such, it localised and physically specified the final aim of moderate nationalism. Again, the initial forms of the Irish Nation overshadowed its future. In the rhetoric of both the repeal movements of the 1830s and 1840s and the Home Rule movements of the 1880s and 1890s 'College Green' (meaning a single familiar edifice) was used as the standard symbol of political restoration.

All this meant that the Parnellite and Redmondite parties were ill-equipped to deal with the problem of 'Ulster'. At any rate they were as unwilling as their northern opponents to regard Ulster as divisible into its predominantly Protestant and predominantly Catholic parts. This would have contradicted both their island image and their received doctrines on the relationship of religion and nationality, and Britain's deployment of sectarianism to divide the Irish. Hence Parnell's gross underestimation of the Ulster opposition of 1885–6. Hence Redmond's timidity and obscurity of purpose when under pressure to concede something on 'Ulster' during 1913, 1914 and 1916. Hence the failure in 1921 of both the Dail Cabinet at home and the Irish plenipotentiaries at the treaty negotiations in London to consider in time the issue of a boundary, and the modes of determining it. Hence even the claim of the 1937 Constitution to be that of all Ireland, and to jurisdiction, albeit prudentially suspended for the time being, over the entire island.

Concretely, the crucial failures were those of 1914 and 1921. Had Redmond and Dillon abandoned, at the beginning of 1914, the mirage of an all-Ireland Parliament and concentrated on gaining for their projected Home Rule government as much of nationalist Ireland as possible, they would surely have been able to secure all or particular areas of every Ulster county except Antrim. By the beginning of July 1914, even Carson was prepared to concede not only Cavan, Donegal and Monaghan but also South Armagh, South Fermanagh and probably South Down in return for a single plebiscite for the remainder of the six 'plantation' counties. Similarly, had Griffith and Collins faced the inevitability of some form of partition in the conditions of late 1921, and concentrated upon the mode of determining where the line should be drawn, they could surely have secured a more or less similar result. In both July 1914 and December 1921 the British negotiators were desperate to find a 'solution' to the immediate problem, and in the second case the northern Protestants posed comparatively much the lesser threat. A proposal to follow the wishes of the local inhabitants in the fringe regions, in so far as this was compatible with a line of division running west from somewhere in Down and south from somewhere in western Derry, would have been defensible in Parliament and in public – indeed it could have been presented as the plainest commonsense; and pressed hard by the Irish delegates, it might well have proved an irresistible temptation, especially at the very end, on the night of 5–6 December 1921.

It seems then a fair conclusion that the respective geographical images of Ulster and Ireland are responsible for the present frontier between the Irish Republic and Northern Ireland. Had the frontier been differently drawn, the history of both would have been very different. Had it been drawn, as seems the most likely variation, so as to include approximately one-third of the present land area and the majority of the districts of Catholic preponderance of Northern Ireland in the Free State or Republic, the 'problems' would certainly have been changed. This is not to suggest for a moment that 'problems' would have vanished. But if the new Irish Free State had to start with the knowledge that the northern Protestants had to be wooed out of their autonomy, were it to govern the whole island; if it had to start with more Protestants in more homogeneous communities within its own bounds; if the new Stormont found itself with a Protestant–Catholic ratio of, say, 3:1 in place of 2:1, and without, or with many fewer, concentrated bodies of disaffected people in its border zone; and if, in the light of this greater security, the Northern Ireland Protestant community could break politically into its component interests, and perhaps even bid for Catholic electoral or party support à la the United Kingdom in 1830–1918 – if all these and many consequential alterations in the basic situation had occurred, Anglo-Irish and intra-Irish relationships would obviously have taken profoundly different courses. The alternative development would not necessarily have been beneficent, in terms of the current liberal (or perhaps any other) concept of the beneficial. Who can say, for example, whether changes in the relative confessional ratios on either side of the border would have worked for or against greater communal accommodation in the end? But this at least can be said: that they would have reflected more accurately in the aggregate the real allegiances, antipathies and sympathies of the Irish population. This is however irrelevant to our present purpose. All I have set out to attempt here is the demonstration of the force of concepts of territoriality in determining very great issues in history.

Of course the very decision of 1921, confirmed in 1925, created in its turn a new mental geography. Once painted a different colour on the map Northern Ireland became a pictorial entity in men's minds, with fresh claims and counter-claims about territoriality. This reinforced the real internal separation of both the Irish Protestant and the Irish Catholic communities, when they were divided between two states, and henceforth carried along, to a degree, in the streams of two separate 'national' histories. Even if only in symbiotic relationship, northern Protestants and Catholics began to have, in certain fields, more in common with one another than either had with their co-religionists south of the border. The new 'Ulster' of the northern Protestants forgot that Donegal, Cavan and Monaghan had ever been part of their province. The Catholics of, say, South Armagh no longer struggled to escape by themselves to Dublin's governance, but rather felt themselves involved forever in the fate of Catholics generally in Northern Ireland. Place, in the political sense at least, had been permanently refocused. Yet the Treaty of 1922 had rendered the northern Unionist view of place more instead of less ambivalent. Had Scotland been a nation-state or even a distinctive kingdom, their difficulty in defining their area in relation to the surrounding world would doubtless have been less. The community, or at least the substantial Presbyterian part of it concentrated in Down and Antrim, might then have seen itself as essentially a colony in the Hellenic sense, though one with unusual frontier difficulties and an unusual division within the ruling class. As things were however neither the Irish nor the British view of insularity or 'islandness' could be consistently embraced; and this geographical insecurity or unease has doubtless increased as the political separation of Northern Ireland from both the remainder of the United Kingdom and the Irish Republic becomes less and less 'unthinkable'. What northern Unionists really mean by 'place' and 'people' is Protestant Ulster. But in terms of the land area of even their state this cannot account for much more than two-thirds of the whole. Yet – apart from anodyne 'Northern Ireland' employable for official purposes – what alternative do they have to 'Ulster'? One cannot very well write Protestant Supremacy upon a map.

IV

Southern unionists, the great bulk of whom were Protestants and who probably in turn accounted for at least nine-tenths of the Protestants of Leinster, Munster and Connacht, had been in a different situation since 1800. For the first quarter of the nineteenth century, their monopoly of power and place, though increasingly under threat, remained secure. This facilitated a dual identity. Their Irishness was established by their very local supremacy and superiority of status, which 'placed' them in all senses. But the fact that this superiority depended not only essentially but even self-confessedly upon British arms and influence made them see themselves as part of an imperial structure. Domestically they were still overlords, but externally they were dependants. Over the next sixty years, 1825–85, however, their standing in Ireland was gradually eroded. This compelled them to modify their traditional view of 'homeland' and 'mother country'.

Despite severe political and economic losses in the middle quarters of the century, the Irish landowning class of the south retained something of their territorial power and influence until very late in the nineteenth century, not least by their continued domination of the grand jury system and thereby of local government in the counties. But thereafter few could fail to see the writing of dispossession (and of the loss of their traditional roles) on the wall. They had to face the fact that, sooner or later, they would be irrelevant in all the crucial matters of life to their own country-side, unless they bent, as most of them never would, to the winds of the new nationalism. Without any longer an Irish *national* function, their Irish identification would inevitably shrink to their immediate locale and, more distantly, to a few surviving Ascendancy institutions such as church and university. On the other hand, their loss of a significant Irish function had been brought about by Britain's surrender of their interests under pressure from their Irish enemies. How to identify with so faithless a mother?

There were no better expositors of the nuances of *fin-de-siècle* southern unionism than Somerville and Ross. Early in the *Reminiscences of an Irish R.M.*, Lady Knox says this of her cousin, the mistress of Aussolas Castle:

She hates all English people. You know the story they tell of her? She was coming home from London, and when she was getting her ticket the man asked her if she had said a ticket for York. 'No, thank God, Cork', said Mrs Knox.

A companion piece comes later in the *Reminiscences*:

> 'When those rascals in Parliament took our land from us', said Mrs
> Knox, flinging a sod of turf on to the fire with practised aim, 'we
> thought we should have some peace, now we're both beggared and
> bothered'.[10]

In comic form these passages express the gentry's alienation from and
resentment of Great Britain at the turn of the nineteenth century. But
there would be no difficulty in finding corresponding bilious comment
from Mrs Knox on the grasping, irresponsible, treacherous natives
amongst whom she and her like were placed. 'Of my nation!', exclaimed
Shakespeare's Captain Macmorris, perhaps the first Anglo-Irishman in
English literature, 'What ish my nation? Ish a villain, and a bastard, and
a knave, and a rascal.' This contempt overleaped the centuries. Of
course, if forced to choose between 'loyalties', the great majority of the
Anglo-Irish gentry would have chosen Britain and Empire. Like the
contemporary officer caste to which they contributed so richly, they had
their symbols, Crown, Country and the like, to sustain them in their
allegiance. The King's ministers or their English 'countrymen' might
abandon or betray them. But their great abstractions stood ever firm.
These served, however, only for the great crises. In the dreary daily
round, they felt little less alienated from their 'mainland' compatriots
than from the surrounding peasantry, priests and publicans.
    In these circumstances, place contracted to familiar topography and
the society of their own kind within visiting compass. Again the *Reminiscences* brings this, in part, to life. The little arc of country at a radius of
20 miles east, north and west from Castletownsend in Co. Cork is
described, both in special instances and in its general air, with exquisite,
loving care. Furze, fuchsia and rhododendron, covert, hill and meadow,
cloud, sky and sea, are remembered with the intensity of a childhood
recollection. The physical precincts were now central to identity. Of
course the Anglo-Irish had no monopoly of the passionate response to
place. O'Connell, to look no further, was quite as strongly bound to his
native peninsula and – as he said himself – 'the calm and exquisite beauty
of these capacious bays and mountain promontories'.[11] But for
O'Connell Kerry fitted comfortably into a nest of Irish identifications. It
was not a solitary survivor.
    But it is not to be supposed that landscape by itself encompassed the
Anglo-Irish world in its final stages. Their Irish location was also, and
perhaps more fundamentally, expressed in terms of the surrounding
Protestant community. Here again Somerville and Ross provide an
insight. Doubtless, the insight was partial and distorting, as any novel-
ist's selection from reality must be. But it is also profoundly revealing of
the underlying assumptions of their caste.

The Real Charlotte (1894) dissects, with great delicacy, the small Protestant society settled about Lismoyle, a dreary rain-washed country town in the south-west of Ireland. It is this community alone which has reality in the novel. Other figures do appear – from an underworld or outworld, so to say. But these servant and peasant types live only as 'sub-people', as a species of animated background. The native population is seen only as children are seen – or rather were then seen – in an adult world; not as developed individuals, but as having a partial, indeterminate existence on the fringe of life.

Thus, 'place' in *The Real Charlotte* is an essentially sectarian phenomenon. Whatever its area, its *meaningful* population is exclusively Protestant. Indeed, it is the Protestant visiting-range or intercourse-district which defines its limits. Yet, seen from within, this 'place' is no stockade or laager but a complex social form. The Big House of the novel, Bruff, is more than *primus inter pares*. But the lesser houses, Charlotte Mullen's Tallyho Lodge, the estate agent, Lambert's, Rosemont and even the *déclassé* Julia Duffy's Gortnamuckla, are neither negligible nor satellites. There is a decided element of gradation in the system. Nor is the Protestant enclave a permanently stratified society. Its ranks are not immutable. On the contrary, it teems with social movement, the struggle for status and esteem within itself rendered, perhaps, all the more desperate by the slow decay and growing insignificance in which all its members were commonly involved. Money emerges as indispensable, if not necessarily sufficient, for social standing. Charlotte mounts in the scale by usury and fraud: Julia Duffy sinks because her progressive poverty cannot be stayed. There is moreover a constant relationship between what happens in Lismoyle and what is happening in a remote exterior world of stocks and shares, of cities and suburbia.

Thus while Ireland, particularised in the imaginary Lismoyle countryside, was the book's physical locale, this locale was *effectively* peopled, for Somerville and Ross, by the tiny Anglican community. This is an important illumination of Ascendancy's adjustment to its new functions, or loss of functions, from the 1880s onwards. For many, their 'place' was practically reduced to their immediate physical surrounds and their neighbouring co-religionists. Of course, the Anglican minority in southern Ireland was not and never had been confined to the landowning or land-managing classes. Especially in the capital, it played a part out of all proportion to its numbers in the upper reaches of commerce and the professions. Throughout the nineteenth century, the middle-class urban Anglo-Irish had been comfortable enough in a sort of social apartheid which had secured them in an Irish 'world', rarely intersecting that of their Catholic counterparts. Their relative insulation from the rest of Irish life did not seriously affect their territorial identification with Ireland in general, and with their town or city in particular. Professor F. S. L. Lyons succinctly bears witness to the change in this condition which began to manifest itself just before the First World War, and was total within a decade.

> After 1921 the arrogance disappeared, but so did the unselfconsciousness. Now on the defensive, the minority became intensely aware of their isolation and withdrew into a kind of ghetto. A ghetto can be just as much a state of mind as a physical locality and if I, as one who grew up in this rather stifling atmosphere, had to say what seems to me the most striking characteristic of the minority in the twenties and thirties, it is the persistence of precisely this ghetto mentality.[12]

Thus, once Home Rule really threatened, still more once the Irish Free State had arrived, the urban Anglo-Irish followed the same path as the gentry and their fellows had taken twenty years before. Their 'place' shrank from a country to a handful of homes and institutions. Like snails, they now carried their 'houses' on their backs; they had lost any larger habitation. Both they and their Catholic fellow-countrymen suffered by this contraction in the first thirty or forty years of the new state's existence. But, relatively speaking, it was a cheap version of decolonisation for an old ruling class; and quite soon a fresh generation of southern Protestants was beginning to repeat the historic processes of accommodation.

V

For Irishmen the issue of Ireland as a place was a particular form of the general question of belonging to a community. In his Dimbleby Lecture for 1982, Dr Garret Fitzgerald defined the Irish problem in terms of where people are born and how they are brought up:

> The sense of identity with a particular community may be given by chance – but it cannot be easily transcended by design. All of us as human beings feel that we must belong, not just to a nuclear family, but to a larger community, which demands a loyalty to it, but gives in response a comforting sense of being part of a greater whole, a wider family of millions.

The late-nineteenth- and early-twentieth-century crisis of the Anglo-Irish derived precisely from the fear – or, if one wishes, the realisation – that their wider family no longer extended beyond the bounds of the island, Ireland. The same is true of the Northern Ireland Protestants at the present day. One can regard the cases as, literally, the internalisation of a problem: or, more exactly, as problems deriving from an enforced internalisation.

By definition, the issue was different for the other party in the conflict. Ireland was very conveniently located on the map, as seen through British eyes. It served like the trick of the tumbling cubes. Change the angle of vision ever so slightly and everything which had seemed to fall in one particular direction now seemed to fall quite as decisively the opposite way. Seen in one geographic light, Ireland could appear as the largest severed part of a single broken land mass 'the British Isles', which themselves took on the form of an occidental Japan or an eastern-Atlantic New Zealand. In another geographic light, however, Ireland could look to be a distinct and independent entity, with the Irish Sea as wide and deep a separating stretch as the North Sea or the English Channel. This provided a useful elasticity. British policy and British opinion could adopt whichever view best suited at the moment.

This is not necessarily to impute hypocrisy or deliberate deceit. People do not generally demand close consistency of themselves. Notoriously, and more or less innocently, they change their definitions, where they can, according to their immediate interest. None the less, it suited very well to be able to see Ireland as integral with Great Britain, or as distinct from her, or as a 'natural' dependency or 'natural' economic satellite or 'natural' military redoubt, at will. The depiction of Western Europe, as laid out familiarly in the mind's eye, rendered such choices easy for those who did not live in Ireland. Their images derived from schoolroom charts, not from daily apprehension of an apparently boundless physical reality.

Thus, in the debate on the proposed union between Great Britain and Ireland in the House of Lords in 1799, the Earl of Minto observed that a glance at the map showed the two islands to be 'not merely contiguous but lying as it were in the bosom and embrace of each other'. Nature had marked them out to be a single state 'not only [by] their mutual vicinity, but [also by] insulation, and their insulation together, from the rest of Europe'.[13] Later, the Marquess of Lansdowne spoke of St George's Channel as a mere canal, the divine equivalent of the waterways then being cut by men throughout the country. Providence had clearly intended the Irish Sea to be, not a dividing water, but 'a glorious navigation' to facilitate traffic between the islands.[14] At the other end of the history of the Union, in 1912, L. S. Amery also called upon the map to justify the junction of kingdoms – adding, after the fashion of the day, some racial and linguistic topping:

Geographically the United Kingdom is a single compact island group, of which Ireland is by no means the most outlying portion. No part of Ireland is to-day, or ever was, as inaccessible from the political centre of British power as the remoter parts of the Highlands, not to speak of the Shetlands or Hebrides. Racially, no less than physically, Ireland is an integral part of the United Kingdom peopled as it is with the same mixture of racial elements as the main island of the group. The blend of Celt with Dane, with Normans and English of the Pale, with English citizens of the seaports and Cromwellian settlers, which constitutes Celtic Ireland, so-called, is less Celtic both in speech and in blood than either Wales or the Highlands.[15]

Conversely, Englishmen had no doubts about Ireland being a distinct physical entity whenever it was advantageous to them to stress the differences in power or people. As an early instance, Swift's *Story of the Injured Lady* (1746), satirising the would-be 'marital' relations of the islands, provides an epitome of the unspoken English assumptions about such differences, when policy beckoned in this direction. In the pamphlet, the English male is piqued that his benevolence in sending the lady so many settlers, striving so hard to teach her manners and providing her with law from on high should be ill-requited. It was but proper that she should not be allowed to contaminate her raw materials by processing or manufacturing them herself. They should serve instead to furnish employment and profit for his own people. There was no question that the islands were not only clearly different things, but also things set in a competitive, indeed, an antagonistic relationship to each other. Englishmen, according to the *Story*'s moral, became geographical separatists the moment their self-interest was touched.

'I write the history of England because it is *normal*', Buckle boasted. His compatriot–contemporaries were never clearer in their minds about the abyss-like character of the Irish Sea than when they thought of Irish abnormalities; and nothing brought this so sharply before their imaginations as law and order. In only sixteen of the first hundred years under the Act of Union was Ireland 'normal' in this regard: 1802, 1805–6, 1812–13, 1819–21, 1829, 1836–42, 1846 and 1872 apart, nineteenth-century Ireland was always subject to a suspension of Habeas Corpus or to a Crimes and Outrages, or a Peace Preservation, or a Protection of Life Act, or to several of these together. In the debates preceding the coercion measures, or the platform thunderings or editorial philippics preceding such debates, there was no allusion to ardent geographical embraces or the providential division of the 'British' land-mass by a 'canal'. True, proximity was not entirely overlooked. But in these contexts, proximity appeared, not as an argument for union, but as an item in the catalogue of differentiation. When disorder and disaffection were the themes, Ireland's propinquity was presented as an additional cause for fear and a heightened reason for repudiating all notions that Great Britain and Ireland constituted a common state or land.

For almost fifty years after the creation of 'Northern Ireland' in 1920, its terrestrial classification presented fewer problems than before to the British visual imagination. At first, truncated Ireland may have looked strange upon the map. But, in time, it came to seem little more anomalous than the Isle of Man. The crucial fact – what rendered it an altered case – was the permanence of a powerful pro-British majority in the newly delineated area. This made it easy to visualise the 'province' as an extrusion of Great Britain, separated from the rest by a mere corridor of water – almost an outlying 'island', even if one half-surrounded by land. Of course, such convenient depictions tended to fade whenever the Northern Ireland minority succeeded in publicising, dramatically, their grievances and discontent. In particular, all images of the geographical integrity of the United Kingdom have been in decline, and those of disjunction in the ascendant, since 1969. But it needed a quasi-civil war to destroy, first, the agreeable notion of the cross-Channel extrusion, and next the old *elasticity* of geographic vision, which had served so well for centuries.

Meanwhile, there had been, to some extent, an ironical role reversal. After 1921 the attitude of people in the twenty-six independent Irish counties towards the remaining six proved not dissimilar to that of Britons to Ireland as a whole, under the Act of Union. When it suited, the geographical integrity of the single island would dominate the nationalist's mental map. But there were times and moods (more frequent, needless to add, in recent years) when such a picture did not suit, when it became imperative to distance oneself from the north-east corner of the Irish land-mass, and to attach significance to its being painted politically another colour. At such times and in such moods, the mind's cubes tumble in the opposite direction, and the boundary stands out, as a weal, marking, not mere county lines, but the start of a different, if not indeed an alien, country. But such a mischievous vision of time's whirligigs as the interchange of the British and Irish stances may imply is perhaps too close to Meredithian Comedy for our century. Meredith's was, relatively, an age of innocence. The Spirit of Comedy, delighting in the very intricacies of human contradiction and absurdity, has long since gone to bed.

Chapter 3

Property

I

The term 'property', as loosely used in nineteenth-century Ireland, carried a double meaning. But the dualism was not immediately apparent. This was so because one version was clearly articulated and expressed precisely in legislation, whereas the other was only to be inferred from agrarian conduct and the coarse clichés of a peasantry. The difference, however, was merely one of accessibility and exactitude of definition. Really, two world-pictures (or at least two societal pictures) of great power and range were in collision, whenever property, and in particular landed property, was being considered.

The first usage was essentially an imported one. The three 'English' revolutions of 1641, 1688 and 1776 had concerned themselves with property and the person; and in combination they had tipped the balance considerably in favour of rights as against obligations, especially amongst the particular 'haves' of the day. The early nineteenth century saw this expressed ever more clearly in both statutory and judge-made law. It also saw a parliamentary and judicial process of equating landed and other types of property advance very rapidly. This advance marched, and was deeply entangled, with the growth of the new science of political economy. To the economists there was at bottom no difference *in kind* between different forms of possessions, however great the difference in accidents or in appearances might be. Moreover, possession was for them an absolute condition. There might of course be joint ownership or partnership in owning. But these merely signified a plurality of possessors, not a diminution in rights; and it was to be assumed that the shares, gains, losses and duties of the possessing parties were readily susceptible to exact apportionment as occasion might require. The political economist went on to import the assumptions that the property-owner would seek to maximise profits from his possession, and that possessions, even landed possessions, should be regarded less as stationary things than as things to be developed. Property was to be seen as dynamic, as the producer of further wealth.

Not only political economy but also – over a much lengthier period – law contributed to the formation of such an atomistic and aggressive outlook. 'Laws foster or create law-making opinion', Dicey once wrote;[1] and the very idea that recent legal developments constituted a progression from status to contract was an important force in the nineteenth century. Maine's *Ancient Law*, published in 1861, best epitomised this notion. But Maine was really summarising in a phrase, and giving a local habitation and a name to something which the preceding generations of Englishmen had cloudily sensed. In particular he was giving meaning and definition to their impression that the trend of statute law, and of a line of appellate decisions in commercial cases stretching back to the seventeenth century, was confirming the essentially individualistic and contractual nature of civil society. Georgian enclosure Acts, the repeal of the Laws of Settlement, the abandonment of prohibitions on the emigration of artisans, the amendment of master and servant legislation and the modification of the Combination Acts, all seemed to represent an uncongealing of society and an advance of individual as against communal rights. Similarly, equity appeared to have turned itself inside out during the eighteenth and early nineteenth centuries, and to have replaced its original purpose of substantial justice by that of formal correctness. In general, equity encompassed the commercial sphere, and the transactions of capital in all its forms fell more or less within its scope; and equitable decisions rested increasingly on the concept of the 'meeting of minds', the inferred formal agreement of specific individual persons or corporations, rather than on any principle of the 'common good' or a higher fairness. Thus Maine appeared to have the support of recent history and contemporary opinion when, looking back, he seemed to see one grand tendency in law over the past century or more, a majestic movement bearing all before it in field after field as it progressed to more sophisticated and 'civilised' social forms. Its essence was the free contract, in entering which all parties were assumed to stand upon a level.

II

The Act of Union in 1801 subjected Irish land – as well as all other Irish affairs – directly to a Parliament where English (I do not even say British) concepts and presuppositions predominated. Initially, this meant the gradual transference of the notions of political economy to the sister island. For the first forty years of the nineteenth century, educated English opinion generally assumed that landownership should be untrammelled *legally* by social obligations or other objects. The good landlord would instinctively shoulder some responsibility for those in his territorial sphere. But defining this responsibility in statute and making it enforceable in law were no more to be thought of than, say, compelling business corporations to set up educational foundations would be today. The philosophy that ownership was, in law, an absolute condition did in fact issue in a stream of Irish land legislation between 1801 and 1840. But these Acts – the Sub-Letting Act of 1823 is a prime example – were designed to secure the landlord's position, as absolute owner, by cheapening and facilitating ejectments, evictions and the consolidation of holdings. They were moreover accompanied by statutory attempts to render these courses of action safer by coercion measures, militia laws, suspensions of Habeas Corpus and other mechanisms for stamping out peasant counteraction.

In the 1840s, partly to counter constitutional agitation, partly to meet the endemic agrarian conflict in the countryside, and partly because of the general, hopeless impoverishment and misery as the country rushed to its ultimate catastrophe of famine, the emphasis gradually changed. Increasingly, the failure of Irish landlordism was attributed to the absence of a system of fully and genuinely contractual relationships in the Irish agricultural economy. The Devon Commission's report of 1845 was the first official acknowledgement that the problem of Irish land was a peasant's as well as a proprietor's problem; and during the great famine of 1845–52 Irish landlordism became discredited among the British public who believed that they were being saddled with relief expenses which the proprietors should have borne. In consequence, the legislation of 1847–9 attempted both to remedy the supposed injustice of the relief costs and to facilitate the transference of Irish land from financially embarrassed landlords to more solvent owners. The Encumbered Estates Act of 1849, which embodied this last objective, has been aptly described by W. L. Burn as an attempt 'to establish free trade in Irish land'.[2] Like all other Irish land legislation between 1845 and 1865, the Act was 'reformist' in the sense that it aimed at making landlord–tenant relationships wholly a matter of 'free contract' (as against status and custom); at eliminating entail and primogeniture and similar clogs upon the purchase and sale of land; and at enabling open competition and the unfettered pressure of supply and demand to establish the 'true' level of rents and the terms of profitable tenancy agreements. The basic principle was clearly expressed in Clause 3 of Deasy's Land Act of 1860: 'The Relation of Landlord and Tenant shall be deemed to be founded on the express or implied Contract of the Parties, and not upon Tenure or Service';[3] and this Act, together with Cardwell's Land Act of the same year, proceeded to set out the covenants implied, unless specifically repudiated, in all such contracts, and to establish mechanisms for determining the respective contractual obligations of the parties, when in dispute.

Thus, the official view of land in Ireland, as it hardened in statutes and judgements during 1801–65, was English derived. The model of real property which it projected became practically indistinguishable from that of personalty. In such a view, land was ultimately like goods, a common-or-garden commodity, which the owner might order as he wished. But in so far as he bargained with another for its use, he contracted in essentially the same fashion as a livery stabler hiring a horse or a grocer selling a pound of sugar.

Of course this was, in one sense, a myth, albeit a myth propounded and defended by the state. It did not describe the reality. Landed relationships in Ireland were often too intricate, even legally, to be amenable to what were, in principle, simple categories. Some landowners were so far removed, physically and psychologically, from their possessions as to render any notion of their economic 'activity', one way or another, quite absurd. Some were no doubt too compassionate to treat their fields and bogs, the very means of survival of the Irish poor, as if they were interchangeable with three-per-cents; others were too fearful of the consequences for themselves or their agents to do so; and others still had mixed motivation for their restraint, or weakness. Perhaps none at all lived up to the image of economic landed man, in its full, iron lineaments.

Moreover, the traditional popular view of the Irish landlords as a rapacious class has been heavily challenged in recent years. There is much evidence, particularly for the years after 1850, that rents often lagged behind prices, that arrears often accumulated, that abatements were commonly allowed in bad seasons and that actual evictions were comparatively rare. There is also some evidence of 'rapacity' by the more moneyed, driving tenants which is supposed to place landlords' doings in a new perspective. It has been argued moreover that the major indictment of the Irish proprietors after the famine should be that they failed to raise their rents sufficiently and to plough back some at least of the additional money into their estates. 'They had failed to exploit rationally the rental capacity of their estates, and they had failed to invest significantly in improvements.'[4]

But none of this – even if we grant it to the full and pass over in silence the assumptions that there were readily discoverable 'proper' levels of economic activity and returns – should be allowed to obscure three leading facts. First, there was a general, abiding conflict of economic interest between landowner and tenant. In Ireland this went far beyond the normal adversary stances of all lessor–lessee relationships, because of the absence there of access to alternative modes of living and because of the cultural and religious antagonisms which were normally added there to the functional and social. Secondly, the overwhelming majority of Irish landlords had neither sympathy with nor understanding of the peasant's view of property. If they ever made concessions from higher motives than pusillanimity, they regarded these as *ex gratia*, not of obligation, and certainly not as derogating from their rights of ownership. Thirdly, however incompletely and with whatever variations of time and place they tried to put them into practice, they were, as a class, deeply influenced by the new English concepts. Ideology and law *did* create a different sort of Irish proprietorial opinion as the nineteenth century unwound, and this *did* affect rural relationships, agricultural production and modes of husbandry.

This last deserves some elucidation. In part, the ideological submission of the Irish landed classes to their British counterparts is to be explained by their loss of control over their own destinies after 1798 – or at least, by their *feeling* that they lost such control, and with it to some extent responsibility for their country and even for themselves. In the united Parliament, their numbers were small and their influence still smaller. They could not stand, even if they wished to do so, against the English and Scottish nostrum-mongers. Especially after 1815, they were marked down as failures in their roles as gentry or magnates; and their failure was soon seen as costly – to the British treasury. The corollary was of course that the piper-payer should call the tune. By the 1820s the Irish proprietors had become, in effect, legislative mendicants, forced to leave the form of statutory alms to the enlightened charity of their fellow-senators. As Cabinets came to dominate in the formulation and passage of parliamentary Bills, and as the doctrinaires came to dominate in many economic questions and debates, so did the standing of the Irish landed classes steadily decline. From the Clare election of 1828 on, they were in the contemptible situation – in Westminster eyes – of not being able even to 'deliver' their own tenants at the polling booths. Thus, English notions of property soon had the Irish field virtually to themselves, at least at the abstract and legislative levels.

Thus even had the Irish Ascendancy been opposed to the trend of Irish land legislation in the first two-thirds of the nineteenth century, their opposition would have had a comparatively small and diminishing effect. But in general they were not opposed. They too were subject to the 'March of Mind' which Peacock satirised in *Nightmare Abbey*. As, by definition, beneficiaries of the process, they began as natural supporters of the absolutist and individualist concepts of property. But their failure of nerve of 1798 and their surrender of their fate to safer hands in 1800 had also general repercussions. A new cultural cringe is detectable in the Ascendancy in the first quarter of the nineteenth century. It was not all a matter of morale. Some of the imitativeness derived from the transformation in the speed of communication between the two islands during the Revolutionary and Napoleonic Wars. Some of it derived from the greater integration of the standards of society in its upper reaches, which led many Anglo-Irish families into a downward spiral of indebtedness and encumbrances. But much was the logical consequence of accepting an inferior, garrison status. The flight for protection to metropolitan power carried with it, in the early nineteenth century, a susceptibility to, even a cowering before, metropolitan opinion.

III

The antithetical or communal concept of Irish land was, like its rival, remote from actuality, and had been so at all periods however distant. But the myth or model of a 'territory' belonging to a group, worked as a means of living and supporting homes rather than for profit, and subject to a customary code of rights and duties, always underlay the peasant attitude. No doubt some even supposed in a hazy way that the model represented the state of things in Ireland before the land seizures of the sixteenth and seventeenth centuries, and looked to such a 'restoration' in their dreams of role-reversal. But well short of so extreme an objective, the communal vision shaped the tenant aims and actions. As Dr Barbara Solow has pointed out, even the formal programme of the Tenant League of 1850, the '3 Fs' (fixity of tenure, free sale and fair rent), was ultimately informed and justified by this body of presuppositions:

> The correct interpretation of the tenant demands is not about divided property rights between owner and tenant . . . but rather concerns a different concept of property altogether, and the issue between land-lord and tenant in Ireland was whether property was to be thought of as private or as in some sense communal.[5]

Much nineteenth-century Irish history then needs an appreciation of the subterranean challenge to the formally dominant theory of property, which the communal vision presented, to be fully understood. To begin with, the agrarian secret societies were, over a century and a quarter at least, deeply influenced by the communal idea. Doubtless still deeper roots might be discovered, but, for working purposes, the Whiteboy movement of the early 1760s may be taken as the originator as well as the archetype of the agrarian combination. The more settled state of Ireland in the mid-eighteenth century had produced two pertinent novelties. First, the anti-Catholic code had been in practice, though not in law, relaxed as the fears of the planters diminished. This in turn restored some measure of Catholic confidence and hope; at the least the former abjectness abated. Although Whiteboyism was not itself sectarian, the vast majority of its participants were Catholics; and its emergence, therefore, depended on a new element of assertiveness on their part. Secondly, agriculture for the market was increasing; and with it the burdens of raised rents, enclosures, spreading pastureage and tithes. In many parts of Ireland these last were borne not by the wealthy but by the poor, by the occupants and the workers and not the owners of the land; and they were correspondingly resented by the victims. It was the fresh, the new, grievances which generated the unwonted resistance.

Whiteboyism, as it swept back and forwards across Munster and south Leinster in its early years, built up a distinctive programme. Although the items and emphasis varied from area to area and from time to time, they formed a coherent whole. The regulation of tithes, leases and rents were of course the most frequent aims. But wages and employment, food prices, county cess, tolls, hearth money and the dues of the Catholic clergy were also areas of conflict. The common element in all these was conservatism – or more exactly perhaps 'preservatism'. Rents, tithes, tolls, taxes, clerical dues and the rest were not assailed in themselves. On the contrary, they were accepted as elements in a received social order. It was innovation and what was seen to be arbitrariness or exorbitance which was resisted. It was the 'moral economy' of the masses, their concept of the right relations between landlord and tenant, farmer and labourer, producer and consumer, purveyor and customer, which they sought to maintain or restore. Moreover, Whiteboyism was not a bargaining affair. Although the bitter foes of unilateral action by others, the Whiteboys fought to impose their own terms unilaterally. The explanation of this, as well as of the enterprise in general, was the communal idea, serving in their minds as a irrefragable justification.

The first agrarian secret societies, Whiteboys and Rightboys, did not discriminate between religions. The main thrust of the movement of 1786 in Munster, for example, was to force Catholic bishops and priests to reduce their ecclesiastical charges; and later the Rightboys even marched over Catholic congregations to services of the Established Church in protest against the demands and conduct of some of their own clergy. It is true that when rural violence reached north Leinster and the Ulster border counties, it turned decidedly sectarian. But it was competition for land, and its corollaries, which had brought the poor Protestant and Catholic tenants into collision. The Protestants were the prime movers, and for them preservation of their 'moral economy' was the driving force. The customary Protestant order, consisting in psychological and political supremacy and systematic economic preference and advantage, was being threatened; and their organisations, the Oakboys and Peep-o'-Day Boys, represented frenzied efforts, by violent popular conspiracy, to restore the status quo. Much the same was true of Orangeism in the succeeding decade, the 1790s. In many respects, the Orange Society (commonly called 'the Orange Boys' at first) was the natural successor of these Protestant Whiteboys. Both were concerned with social and economic dislocation, in the form, this time, of an upheaval from below rather than an imposition from above. It was the same sudden exorbitance and the same vision, or rather nightmare, of role-reversal which brought both into and kept both in being.

So the sectarian variety of rural disorder was also basically conservative in aim. It would be wrong to regard it or its secular counterparts as mere 'protests'. Protests against real or fancied change they certainly were. But it was their special mark to be regulatory and restorative. Many late-eighteenth and early-nineteenth-century observers noted that

Ireland was a peculiarly 'lawless' country. They had in mind not merely the high incidence of agrarian crime – 'criminal' crime, so to say, was generally low – but also the extent to which the legal system of the state was distrusted and abhorred. But the most acute commentators of all, Arthur Young, de Tocqueville and Nassau Senior, went on to emphasise the element of alternative government and alternative law – of a rival legal code and machinery of enforcement – implicit in Whiteboyism and its successors. Thus it would be closer to the mark to describe Ireland as a multi-legal society rather than as a lawless one. The codes developed by the recalcitrant communities had, from their very Whiteboy beginnings in 1761, formal procedures, rules of equity, known scales of penalties and even ceremonies – however grotesque. Of course, violence and conspiracy bred corruption, and these codes repeatedly degenerated. But the *idea* of such a system, expressing and enforcing a superior justice and a surer and fairer retribution than the Crown's justices ever would secure, kept rising out of the particular failures; and it was always vindicated and informed, ultimately speaking, by the vision of the 'true' community.

Of course, the communal idea embraced more than landlord–tenant and owner–occupier relationships. We have seen that religion could sometimes be the basis of conflict between groups fundamentally similar in economic resources (or lack of resources) and that Catholic peasants could turn against their own religion in its material aspects. The anti-tithe movement of the 1830s was to show that a single religio-economic grievance could ostensibly dominate an entire campaign. Again, even the early Rightboys made crude but serious attempts to export their programme beyond a particular district or even county and to embrace an entire class, so far as their tide would run. The Terryalts and Shanavests of the 1810s were really conducting a species of tenant-labourer war. The Ribbonmen, who maintained a shadowy existence in Ulster and north Leinster over the first sixty years or so of the nineteenth century, had general, national and political aspirations, however incoherent and intermittent. Thus, the peasant counter-culture was not directed solely against the landlords and their apparatus. Yet what I have set out in this paragraph are but the minor variations which we should expect in the application of an unrefined popular idea of property to widely differing times and circumstances. The governing concept – not to add, the *modus operandi* – was always essentially the same.

From the mid-eighteenth to the late nineteenth century the communal vision, as practically expressed, did not envisage the elimination of landlordism. The tenant programme never reached, or nearly reached, the height of plain confiscation. There were no suggestions that the land should be simply seized, *à la* France in the 1790s. Nor was there anything to indicate – although this is not of course conclusive – that a successful Irish Revolution would have followed a similar course to the French. It was as if the Irish agrarian masses allowed that their masters had rights roughly corresponding to their own – fixity of home, saleable interest and a reasonable income. This 'reasonable income' might even be described as the surplus product. The tenants never claimed the whole. The landlord was apparently welcome to what was left once all their needs, social, ecclesiastical and familial as well as economic, had been met.

Moreover, in the protracted interchange of the 1880s, as landlordism in general began to weaken, the tenants abandoned co-partnership and adopted individual ownership, rather than communalism, as their goal. There would be no *mirs* in Ireland if they could help it. The final convert and devotee of Political Economy turned out to be, in a sense, the Irish small farmer determined to defend his patch to the death against (as he himself might have put it) every hog, dog and devil that came the road. Yet even in this extremity the idea of community right and justice had not really disappeared. It was rather that peasant proprietorship now offered the ultimate security for the form of rural living which this idea had envisioned.

IV

Thus, we are left with two mutually exclusive and antagonistic versions of the meaning of property in the land; and with each more or less muted and compromised when it came to the actual effort to realise it in ordinary life. This opened the way to grave misunderstanding and crosspurpose, all the more so when, as at Westminster, Downing Street and Whitehall, people quite ignorant of Irish society brought their native categorical frameworks to the consideration of another culture. And even within Ireland itself there were other factors working for misunderstanding and crosspurpose. Chief among these was the original disjunction between peasant and open, constitutional organisation.

The bloody failure of the 1798 rising had broken almost all links between the agrarian conspiracies and the middle-class political groupings. Orangeism may be regarded as a partial exception. But so far as Catholic Ireland was concerned, there was no meeting ground in the years 1800–29. Indeed Catholic politics in the sectarian sense dominated the 'open' political scene in these years; and although such politics were by no means confined to the single issue of the surviving legal disabilities, all else was subordinated to it. Now down to the achievement of 'Emancipation', Catholic politics were the enemy of the secret society, and of the agitation of the land or any other economic grievance. This was true in several regards. First, the campaign strove for a single objective, to concentrate energies and thrust. Secondly, its success depended on the enlistment of the Catholic clergy, to whom the secret oath-bound society was anathema. Thirdly, it could not conduct a parliamentary agitation at all, or an effective agitation of any kind, without specifically and continually repudiating violence and outrage. Finally, the Catholic Association was dominated by men who, whether landowners themselves or not, tended to accept the orthodox, governmental view of property. To look no further than Daniel O'Connell himself, a report of 1822 from his brother James, then acting as his agent for his Kerry lands, makes very clear that he and the peasants were ranged upon opposite sides in a current land war:

[I] left my family in Killarney, took up my residence in the centre of your property and by prompt and energetic measures, I trust, have restored the barony to peace and order. Most of your tenants in this parish were not only affected with the wicked spirit of insubordination now unfortunately so general in the South of Ireland but were actually leaders and principals among the infatuated wretches who composed *Captain Rock's Corps*.

The papers have I presume informed you that seven of those deluded wretches are now in Tralee jail. Jack Douley's son is one of them. Honest Frank made his escape and I candidly confess, though I do not regret his having done so, if he was not in custody I would prosecute him in the same way I will *his friends* that are in jail. I know in times like the present that any man who takes part in putting down an atrocious blood-thirsty rabble who have combined against everything that is respectable in the country, must calculate on the probability of meeting the fate of poor Major Hare, but with respect to myself I am determined at any risk to do my duty . . .

I will scarce be able to make up between this and the assizes your head-rents. Your tenants as well as every other gentleman in Iveragh ate the pigs and beeves and laid out any money they received since 10 of November last (when Captain Rock first made his appearance in Iveragh) in buying clothes and whiskey.[6]

One effect of the Catholic Association's advance from 1823 onwards was the capture of much of the force and some of the techniques of Whiteboyism, and their rechannelling into a parliamentary movement. For a brief period in August and September 1828, between O'Connell's success in Clare and the first clear indication from Wellington that it would actually produce 'Emancipation', there were signs in Tipperary and Armagh that Whiteboyism would break through again. But this was checked successfully. What however was to succeed the Association once 'Emancipation' had been surrendered in 1829?

In fact, despite the apparent dominance of repeal as the issue of the 1830s, the most significant development of the decade was probably the junction of Catholic politics and traditional agrarian resistance in the form of the anti-tithe campaign. Certainly, tithe was a classical Whiteboy

grievance. It was a land charge falling largely upon poor Catholics for the
support of a Church dedicated to the destruction of their own religion.
But it was also an obvious Catholic grievance; and its removal seemed but
a natural corollary, a material expression, of the religious parity which
the Relief Act of 1829 had been supposed to symbolise. Moreover it was
an excellent choice of issue in terms of a British campaign: it would be
difficult to find any element of British power in Ireland which was less
defensible by reason or more assured of British allies, in the form of
insurgent non-conformity.

But the critical thing, in terms of our present interest, was the conver-
gence at last of formal nationalist politics and the peasant counter-
culture. The tithe was in itself a comparatively minor burden; and its
eventual abolition as a direct charge upon the occupier of land was a
rather illusory triumph – much of the imposition crept back as an
element of rent. But meanwhile important new patterns were being laid.
The most interesting of all was the emergence of mass civil disobedience
as a tactic in Anglo-Irish conflict. Patrick Lalor's 'no tithe' movement
was meant to be non-violent. In fact it gained ground when passive
resistance led to considerable bloodshed. It also gained from the unack-
nowledged support of the coercive agrarian societies. But its closest link
to Whiteboyism was the communal vision which it shared. Here was an
entire community mobilised to fight the state – if only with moral
weapons – for one portion of its vision of the just society. It was the
harbinger of the land war of 1879–89, with the state power being employed, ultimately unsuccessfully in each case, to uphold and realise the
absolutist version of property.

At first sight, O'Connell's repeal campaign of the following decade
might seem to have repeated the pattern of the 1820s. The land issue was
submerged in a plain political torrent; and rural disaffection and rude
force were harnessed to an ostentatiously non-violent agitation. In
general, this is fair comment upon the repeal movement, especially for
the years 1843 and 1844. But there were some remarkable new features.
The very organisation of the Repeal Association (even more than that of
its Catholic forerunner) provided a machine for government from below.
The repeal wardens and reading rooms in the parishes formed a rudimentary bureaucratic system, beyond the direct needs of the extra-
parliamentary campaign. In particular, they tried to furnish an alternative or at least a supplementary law and order. Arbitration 'courts'
determined disputes over land rights and duties, and the wardens acted
so far as might be as a species of independent, autonomous police. Not
only did this prefigure, however roughly, the Sinn Fein campaign of
1919–21, but it also expressed in a new and 'civilised' form the historic
moral economy of the peasant masses. It was their concept of property
and community which was being projected in the new sub-government –
at least internally, for the Association stopped well short of any direct

challenge to the landlords or the Crown. But even here, in terms of the state proper, there was an unspoken threat. Indeed it might be said to have been 'spoken' in the end, when O'Connell projected the Council of Three Hundred. This popular assembly was, in idea, the ultimate, national expression of the self-regulating community.

The third stage in the interpenetration of the subterranean economic and the open political movements was reached after (and in part because of) O'Connell's failure and disappearance from the scene and the effects of the great famine in riveting attention on the land issue. The Tenant League of 1850 at last solemnised the marriage of the land and constitutional agitation, after the oblique courtships of the two preceding decades. Its set programme, though outwardly seeming a sober log of claims, was also an attempt to cast in terms of the heads of parliamentary bills the ancient dreams and passions of the landed poor. The '3 Fs' (fixity of tenure, free sale and fair rent) are well worth analysis.

V

The first of the three objectives in the programme of the Tenant League, fixity of tenure, seemed in flat contradiction to the received idea of property in Britain. How could a tenant have a 'right' to occupancy if he did not fulfil the conditions of the contract which had placed him on his holding? But the Irish tenant was pursuing a line of reasoning which never intersected the atomistic–contractual. It was perfectly true that the claim to fixity of tenure implied a 'right' to occupancy. But the context of such a claim in Ireland was a world apart from that used in parliamentary debates. By fixity of tenure the Irish peasant meant that the tenant could not be removed because he was inefficient, or undeferential, or disgruntled, or a Catholic, or defiant in voting against his landlord's direction. None of these was regarded as a proper reason for uprooting a man and his family from the soil in which, Anteus-like, they had 'grown' and 'grew'. Eviction for non-payment or even for arrears of rent was allowed – but only *in extremis*. Not merely would the failure to pay have had to be prolonged, it would also have had to be *culpable*. This was the critical test: from each according to his capacity. The tenant who kept back the customary charge for land-use from mere cupidity was fair game, but not the tenant who would be distressed in a particular season or run of seasons if he strove to meet the entirety of his legal obligations.

Correspondingly the second 'F', free sale, undoubtedly implied a degree of co-possession between the lessor and lessee. Of course, this was anathema to the orthodox early Victorian economist or jurist. But again the Irish context was a world apart from his. The tenant did presume that he had a certain property in the property, but he saw this property as essentially hereditary and usufructuary. In part, his claim was grounded in his sense of the family chain linking the past and future generations. He believed it to be but 'natural' that he should transmit – or at least be enabled to transmit – his holding to his heirs in the same fashion as the proprietor would pass down his demesne to his successors. The tenant also saw himself as mingling his labour with the earth which was temporarily in his charge, and thereby establishing a saleable interest by his very tenure. If therefore he were removed or wished to leave, he felt that his investment of time and effort should be rewarded. He was not ordinarily a mobile or a sterile person, but if he had to move, or had no child to step into his place, he did not see why his 'patrimony' and all his care and labour should be treated as so much mere writing on the water.

The last 'F', fair rent, was overtly uneconomic in character, as contemporary political economy viewed such things. It implied that rent should not be determined merely or even mainly by market forces, but rather by what the sitting tenant could afford. The deciding factor in rent levels should be the tenant's capacity to pay after subtracting what he needed for a reasonable mode of living for his family and himself – not the utmost that the landlord could secure, or what the landlord might require for his particular needs. Again, the tenant, so fiercely hostile to the unilateral determinations of others, was insistent on unilateral determination by his own group. Nor did he see himself or his fellows as arbitrary or aggrandising when they decided what he could afford. As he saw it, it was from the community that the answer to 'what is needed for a reasonable mode of living?' would well up. This was his moral authority.

Had the true derivation of the '3 Fs' been elaborately set out, they could scarcely have achieved a hearing in the Westminster of the 1850s and 1860s. In the social model from which they sprang, the significance of land and labour was not primarily economic. There was 'no way for land allocation to be completely efficient'.[7] The market forces could not *per se* replace the idle or ignorant tenant by the industrious and able, or achieve economies of scale, or alter the technology employed. Not only could profits not be maximised but also this would be no one's aim. Had all this been frankly stated, it would have been hooted or hallooed out of court. But using a language of individual rights, and specifying three apparently clear legislative objectives, at least brought the programme into the arena of the debatable.

It is true that the Tenant League was not quite devoid of economic theory. In the two decades before its birth, a handful of Irish publicists had argued for one or other of its tenets. In 1830 William Conner had proposed that rents be fixed by arbitration instead of competition. He had also advocated absolute security of tenure subject to the payment of the fixed rent. From 1835 onward, Sharman Crawford was pressing the tenant's right to compensation for improvement. In 1836 William Blacker set out a justification of Irish small-holdings on *economic* grounds. If, he wrote, their tenants had 'durable and certain interest'[8] in them, the other basic Irish desiderata, social security and conditions favourable to capital accumulation, would certainly follow. A decade later, James Fintan Lalor pointed to the interrelationship of social, economic and political revolution, land tenure being the nodal point. But these men were mere Irish small proprietors, land-agents or farmers. True, their daily experience taught them the realities of the Irish countryside, and their speculations were rooted in felt and perceived Irish need. But in British eyes they were at best (Crawford partly excepted) obscure scribblers, with no claim to speak from within political economy.

It was not until 1865, fifteen years after the opening of the Tenant League agitation, that any of its programme found academically respectable support. Even then an Irish birth and residence were needed to produce the crucial break with orthodox economics. J. E. Cairnes, born in Co. Louth in 1823, occupied in Galway in the early 1860s the second of his three chairs of political economy – the first having been the Whately professorship at Dublin University. In 1865 he burst forth as an advocate of peasant proprietorship. Cairnes now saw 'property' in land as qualified, not absolute. In particular, he argued that those who put labour into land thereby acquired a 'right' to share in the fruits of their work. Although this fell short of the full '3 Fs' it was imbued with their spirit. Distantly, it even invoked the corporate idea.

Cairnes was already widely known and among liberals at least warmly admired for his work, *The Slave Power*, in defence of the northern states in the American civil war. His 'conversion' on the Irish land issue was to be rendered still more significant by his translation to the chair of political economy at London in the following year 1866. Not only did this mean a move to the metropolis, but also it allowed him to extend his influence over his radical economist friends, J. S. Mill (now his near neighbour), Henry Fawcett and L. H. Courtney. Mill had long been trumpeted as a 'progressive' on the Irish land issue. But this was misleading. His teaching had amounted to little more than support for 'home colonisation' or settling the surplus population on waste land, as a preliminary to establishing capitalistic farming in the 'cleared regions'. But now he followed Cairnes's ideological leap. *England and Ireland*, published in 1868, broke with the notion that ownership was a condition of absolute rights. It also broke with the notion that England represented an economic norm or model: 'No one', he told the House of Commons in the same year, 'is at all capable of determining the right political economy for any country until he knows its circumstances.' [9] Once more, the corporate idea was an ultimate, if also distant and unspecified, source of the volte-face.

It was a short step from this abandonment of contractualism by the left to a confused retreat from its full rigours by Parliament. Gladstone's Land Act of 1870 was presented as wholly orthodox, that is, as upholding the accepted rights of property; and as such its passage through both Houses was quite smooth. At first sight, it seemed comparatively harmless. It merely rendered statutory the tenant's right to sell his 'interest' in his holding wherever this was already customary in Ireland (that is, in parts of Ulster); compensated the evicted tenant for disturbance, according to a fixed scale of damages, unless the cause of eviction was non-payment of rent; and provided compensation for the evicted tenant's improvements even where he was evicted for non-payment. Practically, these provisions produced little or no change in Irish landed relations. At most, they legalised the extra-legal actuality. But the ineffectuality of the measure should not lead us to miss the revolution in principles which it set off.

The right to compensation for improvements made without the landlord's consent; the qualification of his powers to evict; and the statutory endorsement of a tenant's right to sell an 'interest' in his land, all contradicted the shibboleth of unbridled landlord control over his own property. Their corollary was of course that Irish landed property was no longer wholly private. The tenant now possessed legal extra-contractual rights, calculable in money terms, in the soil he tilled. The landlord could not deal with his 'own' entirely as he wished. The mid-Victorian orthodoxies had begun to crumble.

The 1870 Act was the product, not of Irish agitation, but of a general compact between Gladstone and the Irish Liberal–nationalists. But when, from 1879 onwards, the storm of tenant resistance rose with the threat to their living standards, the effects of the earlier erosion were immediately apparent. The Land Act of 1881 fully adopted the '3 Fs'. It provided security of tenure, no matter what the nature of the original agreement; it empowered the tenant freely to sell whatever interests he might have acquired in the property; and special land courts were to determine 'fair rents' to replace the current rentals. The 1881 Act was thus an undisguised acceptance of co-ownership. 'Free contract' was wholly abandoned, to be replaced essentially by status; and the state was to be permanently involved in the conflict between the wrangling partners through the institution of the land courts, enjoined to fix 'judicial rents'.

As we should expect, co-ownership proved to be an unstable condition. For example, what was to be the response to the massive accumulated arrears of rent under the new circumstances? The answer (as again we should expect, though it came as a thunderbolt to Victorians) was that the state should meet the bill. The Arrears Act of 1882 cleared tens of thousands of holdings of debt by paying £2 million of public money to the landlords. Moreover, the land courts, although presided over by judges, were far from judicial, as the word was then understood, in their determinations. Well before the first sat, the tenants were told by the Land League that the level of rents set would depend on the extent of the civil commotion which they created. So it proved. 'Judicial rents' were essentially 'political rents', and the judges essentially ministerial conciliators and public appeasers. Inevitably, as this war of pressures began to seem endless, and the intervals between the fixing of rents diminished, the state moved towards the elimination of landlordism altogether. A succession of land purchase Acts in the later 1880s and the 1890s culminated in Wyndham's Land Act of 1903 by which the government undertook the acquisition and reallocation of estates, with lavish cash bribes to the proprietors and the bribe of low interest rates and lengthy repayment periods to the tenants. A process of dispossessing a once-ruling class, even if most tenderly, was well under weigh.

There are of course abundant ironies, not to say ambiguities, in all this. At one level, ideology was responding to, and changing in accordance with, political pressures. The late 1880s were the climacteric for the Irish landowning class. Somewhere in those years their ultimate ambition for their properties began to change from possession to cashing-in on favourable terms. The commercial revolution, once the sharpener of their acquisitiveness and spur to profits, had overtaken them with a vengeance! Despite the partial success of the last-ditch landlord resistance of the 1890s, in the Property Defence Association and similar counter-organisations, the proprietors were really being worn down by a land war of attrition. Indeed, the final defiant militancy of 'property' probably hastened its end, for clearly such extraordinary exertions and expenditure could not be sustained. If these were necessary to hold even a little ground in mid-Tipperary and West Waterford, the case was surely hopeless.

But the Irish landlords despaired not so much because of their defeats at home as because of the Irish tenant gains in the sphere of metropolitan opinion. As Mrs Knox had tartly summed it up, 'those rascals in Parliament took our land from us'. Here was a second irony. Just as they had been elevated and inspirited in the earlier nineteenth century by English political economy and law, so now the Irish proprietors were being rejected and (as they would have said) betrayed by the turnabout in both, for which the Irish peasant offensive could largely claim the credit. One says both political economy and law, because legal orthodoxy was being equally subverted. The land courts instituted in 1881 created extra- (and perhaps also pseudo-) judicial roles for the judiciary. Their new work was, at bottom, both theatrical and political. In its exercise they were subjected to incessant organised pressure, in form of continued land agitation. In fact, the late Victorian arbitration system, which the land courts represented, might even be regarded as Star Chamber redivivus, with public policy being advertised and particularised rather than decided by legal instrumentalities – except that the driving force was now mass rather than royal power.

More significant still, the very notion of this arbitration system eschewed contractualism in favour of the concept of an inherent 'just price' for land; while in practice this 'just price' was largely set by the community concerned – by the threat, as well as the actuality, of its violence and disturbance. Thus beneath the veneer of neutral legal determination, based on professionally assessed values for acreages and tenements, the communal vision – prudentially modified and unarticulated – was finally triumphant. The 'judicial determination' was in essence a registration of popular will. The values set upon land and buildings were in the last analysis the social values of the Irish countryside, the traditional estimates of right relations between owner, occupier and worker, and of their familial needs.

We have spoken earlier of the irony of the communal vision's ending in an absolute view of property and ownership on the part of the small farmer-proprietor. But even here ambiguity was heaped upon ambiguity. In certain senses and places, and particularly in the old Congested Districts, peasant proprietorship was but the legal carapace for communalism. This communalism did not spring from any new collectivist impulse. Rather it re-expressed, in the new economic structure of myriad owners, the ancient concepts of mutual obligation and dependence.

The Irish Free State Census of 1926, the first to be taken in nationalist Ireland after the virtual completion of land reform, enumerated 268,000 farmers and only 113,000 agricultural labourers. But it also listed 264,000 persons as 'relatives assisting farmers', most of them on tiny holdings. If we add to these persons, the wives and young children who were also crucially involved in the farm economy, it is at once clear that the great majority of Irish agriculture was being run by petty familial co-operatives. Despite the pattern, seventy-five years old, of the regular migration of younger sons and daughters to the towns, across the Channel or overseas, a very large number still remained as semi-dependants, semi-employees, in their original homes. Small wonder that Arensberg and Kimball in their celebrated anthropological study *The Irish Countryman* employed the term 'familialism' to describe Irish rural society in the early 1930s.

But they also found that communalism stretched well beyond even this extended family economy. In particular the general practice of 'cooring' effected co-operation on an extra-familial and neighbourhood basis. As Terence Brown puts it, 'cooring' was

> a deeply-felt system of obligation in the exchange of services and implements between individual households. The only interruption to this strictly familist social system was the help proffered to individuals who could not be expected to reciprocate in any way. A widow, for example, trying to keep her farm together with the help of hired hands could expect a local family to help her out at harvest time, but again the impulse was not at all collectivist, but, in such instances, charitable. [10]

Thus, more than a century and a half after it was first embodied in a peasant programme, the communal vision was briefly realised, so far as such things can be, in the Irish countryside. Paradoxically, it was achieved, in formal terms, by the multiplication, many hundredfold, of the number of absolute owners in the land. But this was a mere paradox, nothing more. The apparent contradiction was only a thing of surfaces; and the underlying reality was well in keeping with all the illusions, double purposes and cross meanings whereby an economic revolution and a social counter-revolution had been, gradually and painfully, accomplished.

Chapter 4

Politics Pacific

I

Paradoxically, an inquiry into the ambivalences of nineteenth- and early-twentieth-century Irish constitutional politics is best begun by some consideration of their British counterparts. This is because of the 'union' which subsisted between the two islands down to 1922, and for another fifty years, if not to this very hour, between the entirety of one island and the north-eastern corner of the other. For the Act of Union between Great Britain and Ireland which came into force on 1 January 1801 was, and remained – and so far as the six northern counties of Ireland are concerned still remains – an act of ambiguity, not to say self-contradiction. Ostensibly the union was a junction of kingdoms. In fact, after two or three years of confusion, the separate British executive was retained in Dublin, after the fashion of a Crown colony. It was not to be expected that Irish opinion could influence the conduct of this form of government. The representation of Ireland at Westminster in 1801 was much less than half what it should have been on the basis of relative population; and it was still practically confined to, and practically controlled by, the collaborationist Anglican Ascendancy. No serious collision of interests seemed possible.

Even had the Irish MPs been hot-eyed republicans instead of loyalist landowners and lawyers they would have been hopelessly outnumbered. As Arthur Griffith put it, melodramatically, more than a century later, '103 Irishmen in the House of Commons face 517 foreigners . . . [on a] battleground . . . chosen and filled with Ireland's enemies'.[1] But this was of course quite remote from the reality. Even in parliamentary terms the road of nineteenth-century change had led not to 103 but, at the highest and most extravagant computation, to 85 Irish intransigents in the House of Commons; and their most absolute enemies there were the remaining 18 Irish members.

Formally, then, the Act of Union had reduced Ireland to a geographical expression within the United Kingdom. But its separate governmental system restored it *sub rosa* to provinciality or colonyhood. Correspondingly, the logic of a common Parliament was common membership of parties covering the entire British Isles. But the fact that the great bulk of Irishmen were regarded and came to regard themselves as a people held down by force ensured that their representatives could never merge completely with the British parties. The Irish Nationalist

MPs were thus inherently prone to opposition, not merely to the ministry of the day, but also to the entire parliamentary structure in which they would always constitute a more or less inassimilable fragment. There was therefore an important gap between theory and practice in Ireland's constitutional situation after 1800, and especially so after the electoral revolution of 1826–8 which clearly established that absolute Ascendancy control of the Irish county constituencies, at least, could be broken. In short, whereas the fundamental *legal* implication of the Act of Union was equality between, and parity of treatment for, the inhabitants of the two islands, the Act's fundamental *political* purpose was anti-separatism; and this had become, by the 1830s, virtually synonymous with resistance to the Catholic majority in Ireland. As the relative power of the Catholics to harm increased, so did their nature, as a subservient and inherently inferior race, occidental orientals in fact, became clarified in British minds.

Legislatively, too, *unequal* treatment of the two islands proved imperative. In such crucial features of the 'age of improvement' as parliamentary and local government reform, church and educational reform, the poor law and police, Irish and English legislation diverged increasingly. The Reform Act of 1832 left all the Irish half-rotten and half-pocket boroughs intact, and increased the total Irish representation by a mere five seats – one of which had gone to the Tory stronghold, Dublin University, and another to Belfast. In local government, the Irish Grand Jury Act of 1837 largely confirmed the enormous powers of the indigenous landed proprietors, at a time when the English justice of the peace was yielding ground at many points. The Irish Municipal Reform Act of 1840, abolishing most corporations, emasculating the few survivors and setting a very high £10 qualification for the franchise, contrasted sharply the equivalent English Act of 1835 which had rendered the towns and cities so many bastions for the middle and lower-middle classes. The 'spoliation' of the Church of Ireland began in 1834 just as the Church of England was setting out upon a new course of vigour and renewal. State-aided elementary education, as a means of mass indoctrination against 'disorder', was launched in Ireland in 1831; it was not considered necessary in England. Though the new police and the new poor law were at first structurally similar in the two countries – in the first case Ireland provided the original model, in the second, England and Wales – they developed upon very different lines. The Irish police constituted, willy-nilly, a paramilitary force, while the Irish poor law could never attempt to deal with such questions as unemployment, with which the English was essentially concerned – what would not be required of a workhouse system tackling unemployment in a country where anything between a quarter and a half of the entire population might be effectively workless at any time? Thus the 1830s and 1840s were marked by increasing divergence in the formal social arrangements of Great Britain and Ireland. In a phase of massive constitutional and institutional change, the very different realities of the two islands enforced very different treatments. The same body controlled the legislative process for both, but in the case of Ireland its fundamental object was the maintenance of imperial control.

Yet this divergence, in its discriminatory aspect at any rate, could not endure. The very factor which had worked against parity in the second quarter of the nineteenth century worked in the opposite direction during the last. By then Catholic–Nationalist power had grown prodigiously in the Irish countryside and in the House of Commons, and the outworks of the system of indirect rule through the Protestant minorities in Ireland had been reduced by decades of bombardment. In the end, killing Home Rule by kindness seemed to be the last *attacking* card left in the hand of even – or rather especially – the Unionist Party. Faced by the later 1880s with the steady demonstration that four-fifths of the Irish constituencies were prepared to endorse *ad infinitum* the demand for a substantial, if ill-specified, measure of autonomy, the British political classes had to find some comforting explanation. For quite as important as the continued workability of the parliamentary system was the British – or more precisely the English – self-image. Two decades earlier in 1867 Salisbury could pronounce, in marmoreal phrase, 'Ireland must be kept at all hazards; by persuasion, if possible; if not, by force'.[2] Those days were over. The naked needs or supposed needs of power could no longer satisfy English *amour propre*, let alone be publicly enuciated. So Irish political disaffection had to be attributed to social, religious or economic imparity, with the corollary of 'positive discrimination' in terms of land tenure, state investment in economic development, Catholic education, and the like – anything rather than place Irish nationalists on a level in terms of political choice. Such were the last refuges of the Tories. But once the third Home Rule Bill was introduced in 1912, the successive tergiversations of Asquith's government, and in particular the double standards exhibited in the Curragh, Larne and Howth episodes in 1914, made it clear that the racial presuppositions of the Liberals were not in the end so very different from the Conservatives'.

Thus, Lloyd George's famous gibe that to negotiate with the Irish was to try to pick up mercury with a fork might also have characterised the Irish nationalist conception of the brother island. One says 'brother' because, significantly, the sexual image was in constant use in nineteenth- and early-twentieth-century England to express the dominator's concept of the relationship between the two islands – with perhaps the later Land Acts dimly perceived as a sort of counterpart to the Married Woman's Property Acts, and the British retention of the power of political decision subconsciously validated by similar psychological mixtures of assertion and insecurity! Even the Hibernophiles might explain themselves in terms of arch-femininity. Harold Begbie, the *Daily Chronicle* journalist, introduced his Home Rule tract of 1912 with Ireland a young and capable matron seated at her fireside, who raises her grey eyes to the visitor, and says with a whimsical and ingratiating play of laughter on her lips, 'I wish to do my own housekeeping; I think I can do it in a better way, and more cheaply, than other people can do it for me. I have no desire to fall out with my neighbours, no inclination to remember old scores against them.'

The old gentleman next door may be alarmed by this ambition, but the lady has really no more evil intent against his prosperity than to sell him the surplus of her butter and eggs.[3]

Analogy, then, compounded ambiguity in the British attitudes.

Let us try to summarise the consequences of these attitudes for Irish politicians. The Union of 1801 had come about for reasons of security – strategic and international in the case of Britain, domestic in the case of the Anglo-Irish Ascendancy. This was covered over by its statutory formulation as a compact entered into by free parties. But the implication of the 'contract' that henceforward all laws would be common to the two islands could not stand against the need for greater coercion and control in Ireland, if she were to remain 'secure'. Nor could it stand in an era of liberalising and devolutionary reform. Modest enlargement of the area of shared power in Britain might strengthen rather than weaken the constitutional structure. In Ireland the opposite would happen. Hence the increasing hollowness of the notion, union. Yet, in the long run, and especially after the passage of the second Reform Act in 1867, Griffith's 517 'foreigners' in the House of Commons constituted, so to say, their own Achilles' heel, because they were divided into major parties struggling for office. Parnell once said that the autocratic government of Ireland was not impossible, nor even particularly difficult, but that the two-party system in Great Britain ensured it would never come about. Once the Nationalist members were sufficiently compacted and numerous to control, at certain junctures, the balance of power, the 517 were no longer a security against all Irish pressures.

This meant that in some respects Ireland had moved from a disadvantaged to a privileged position within the United Kingdom by the close of the nineteenth century. A very striking instance is her retention of 103 MPs when the membership of the House of Commons was redistributed in 1885, for by then 103 MPs for Ireland constituted gross over-representation. The payment of Irish rent arrears by the state in 1882; its provision of loans and grants for Irish rural economic development; and its financing of Irish land purchase, ultimately upon a comprehensive and national scale, all went far beyond what Westminster would have been willing to furnish for the remainder of the United Kingdom in the years 1880–1910. But once more this was imparity, not union. The 'union' might still present itself to Englishmen in the marital image – except that the aggrieved and contumacious wife had at last nagged her way to an avalanche of concessions. But of course such a metaphor covered only one British mood and only one British mode of expounding the relationship. At other times or in other circumstances, the common culture, common services and common obligations of the two islands held the stage, while in others still it was need for a very different apparatus of law and repression in Ireland which dominated.

Thus ambivalence continued to reign in the British attitudes to which Irish nationalism had to respond. It was a vital, though perhaps also an ultimately impossible, matter to master the multi-layered language of Westminster and Whitehall, and to decipher the code which embodied the complex and shifting roles in which current British necessity cast the Irish malcontents. Why was this vital? Because, to quote T. P. O'Connor once more, Ireland under the Act of Union represented the government of one people through the public opinion of another. It was British opinion, and in the last resort British opinion working in British domestic politics, which produced political change in Ireland. From stage to stage, the fashionable Irish tactics altered, from mollification to violent outrage, and back again, and intermingled. But the strategic iron law – that all words and actions were ultimately to be evaluated in terms of their effects upon neighbouring opinion – endured. From O'Connell's efforts to construct alliances with the Whigs in 1835 to the bloody ambushes of 1920, it was English feeling which represented the target and the prize. It is this above all which explains why the exterior set of ambivalences is crucial to explaining the internal.

II

Let us take up the analysis of internal ambivalence at 1830 when O'Connell launched his first serious campaign for the repeal of the Act of Union. For in ambiguity as in so many other aspects of the emerging Catholic nation, O'Connell blazed the Irish trail. The first salient fact of his parliamentary career is that he commenced it after thirty years of practice at the bar. He accepted 'the law' unquestioningly as the legitimate circumscriber of political thought and action; and behind this acceptance of the 'lawful' lay an acceptance, again as a datum, of all the institutions of the state. O'Connell's abhorrence of what he himself called 'physical force' doctrines may also have flowed from his legalism. It must be allowed that his various experiences of revolutionary violence in the 1790s (uncomfortably close to first hand) may have worked in the same direction. None the less, his habitual obeisance to the lawful blocked for him any avenue of thought which might have led to even the contemplation of a *forcible* disturbance of the received order. Conversely, the lawyer–agitator was tempted constantly to consider (and often to test in practice) the legal brinks and borderlands. Such was the mind and habit which this particular liberator brought to a struggle for national independence.

Why did he cast his struggle into one for repeal of the Act of Union? Literally interpreted, repeal was politically nonsensical. The 'Grattan's Parliament' which was being sought had rested on the bases of British political control (which had in turn depended on corruption) and Irish Protestant engrossment of local power and office. By 1830 both, in their pre-1800 forms, lay in that overflowing receptacle, the dustbin of history. It would have been quite impracticable to reconstitute the Irish Parliament in the 1830s without admitting a possible nationalist majority in the lower House. Exterior British control of an Irish Cabinet was equally impracticable for the same reason, namely, that it could not prevail against a hostile parliamentary majority. Moreover, any body dominated by O'Connell was bound to press for the full radical programme of parliamentary reform, down even to universal male suffrage and equal electoral districts. He himself described the six points of the People's Charter as 'ancillary to and promotive of the great cause of repeal'. It was therefore with some justice that Isaac Butt, later to invent Home Rule but at this stage the rising hope of the stern, unbending unionists, contended that

> Repeal was a revolution.... The proposition was not to return to any state of things that previously existed in Ireland — not to adopt the constitution of any European state, but to enter on an untried and wild system of democracy.[4]

Why, then, repeal? The answer is, I think, that O'Connell did not intend it as a specific proposition or demand. It was rather, in lawyer's language, an invitation to treat, an attempt to *elicit* a proposition from the British government. This is confirmed by O'Connell's repeated provision of an alternative which stopped short of formal separation of any sort. When he renewed (one might almost say, originated) his campaign for repeal in 1840, it was through the medium of a National Association of Ireland for Full Justice or Repeal. On the face of things, the inclusion of the alternative 'Full Justice' was inexplicable. O'Connell had, of course, an 'explanation'. He argued that if the 'English' people wished to destroy him politically they had merely to deprive him of supporters by granting Ireland equal justice. But he added that such justice was so clearly *not* going to be conceded that the Association's one and only true aim was repeal; and he 'strenuously denied' that the alternative in the title of the organisation meant that he was not in earnest about the more radical objective. Similarly, 'Full Justice' was an elastic term for O'Connell. At the initial meeting of the Association he had said that 'if Ireland were given the 176 members of Parliament she was entitled to, he would give up Repeal';[5] but later his list of the inequities needing to be rectified was long and detailed. All this really amounted to an oblique expression by O'Connell of his readiness to bargain, if possible with the Whig government (or, after mid-1841, a Whig opposition), and failing that to bargain at least with the Irish Liberals for a common front.

Nor did the disappearance of 'Full Justice' from the Association's title in 1842 mean an end to the ambivalence or concealed invitation to do business. For repeal was only *apparently* a demand. In reality it represented the sloganising of pressure designed to force out a counter-offer, as is apparent in this extraordinary passage at the close of the speech in which he launched the great repeal campaign of 1843:

> a Parliament inferior to the English Parliament I would accept as an instalment...if it were offered me by competent authority. It must first be offered me — mark that — I never will seek it....I will never ask for or look for any other, save an independent legislature, but if others offer me a subordinate parliament, I will close with any such authorized offer and accept that offer.[6]

Like his successors from Parnell to Griffith, O'Connell was a separatist whose measure of separation would be ultimately determined in Great Britain. His demand, like theirs, was therefore expressed in apparently precise and precedented, but essentially meaningless, abstractions.

Here then we have a prime and classic case of our phenomenon. Repeal met all the requirements for mass agitation. Ostensibly no objective could be clearer, or *mechanically* simpler to obtain: a single, short, reversing Act of Parliament seemed sufficient. As a vehicle on which current wrongs and miseries could be heaped, there was no limit to repeal's capacity; and instead of an impossiblist isolation, it promised an almost equally satisfying parity. Significantly, in one of his rare elaborations of repeal to his Irish public, O'Connell envisaged *three* Parliaments, an Irish, a British and an imperial, consisting of both sets of members. The crucial feature was not the degree of independence of the Irish Parliament, but its equality of standing, its identical measure of dependence, with the British. Conversely, the repeal movement appeared to fit a pattern of constitutional agitation, to which the British public had become habituated. It differed profoundly from Chartism in its rigid structure and discipline, its parliamentary capabilities, and its seemingly negative character, as a mere abolitionist organisation aiming at the restoration of a status quo. Above all the proposed return to 1782 permitted the notions of political independence and of fervent adherence to the throne (and with that a sort of general absolution for all other extravagances) to coexist, and even be specifically connected. No contemporary appears to have remembered that the appeal from evil ministers and Cabinets to the misadvised Crown itself had been the first decisive move towards revolution in the Netherlands, North America and France.

In short, repeal was the paradigm of ambiguity in constitutional nationalism. True, the entire web of delicately contrived impressions was roughly torn away when in October 1843 the culminating repeal meeting at Clontarf was proclaimed. Then, the entire movement withered on the vine. But this was in many ways a chance success for repression. Had O'Connell and Peel possessed less control over their respective followers; had (as might well have been the case) the decision of the law officers on the legality of the proclamation gone the other way; had (above all) O'Connell not been so well known, had his characteristics and devices not been so long exposed to the scrutiny of his opponents, there might well have been quite a different ending to the great campaign.

III

Essentially, Parnell and Home Rule was the evening performance of O'Connell and repeal. No men could have been more different in superficial personality and technique, the one a master of verbosity, elucidation and the theatrical, the other, of silence and repose. Their milieux too differed profoundly, quite apart from the fact that Parnell had land to till which O'Connell had had first to map. Yet Home Rule, in Parnell's hands in the 1880s, had all the apparent solidity but actual plasticity of repeal in the 1840s. True, forty years of agitation had driven back the British outworks. It was comparatively safe for Parnell, unlike O'Connell, to indulge in platform sedition. At the threshold of his great decade, early in 1880, he told an American audience, according to one account,

> When we have undermined English misgovernment we have paved the way for Ireland to take her place among the nations of the earth. And let us not forget that that is the ultimate goal at which all we Irishmen aim. None of us, whether we be in America or in Ireland . . . will be satisfied until we have destroyed the last link which keeps Ireland bound to England.[7]

He could always present his parliamentarianism as conditional: 'if our constitutional movement were to fail I would not continue one hour at Westminster'. In his final days, shortly before his death in 1891, he moved back closer to pseudo-violence. 'I have not misled you,' he declared in Dublin, 'I have never said that the constitutional movement must succeed . . . if Ireland leaves the [constitutional] path upon which I have led her . . . I will not for my part say that I will not accompany her further.'[8] Yet, as F. S. L. Lyons observes, even as he spoke these words, 'the familiar ambiguity remained . . . he still continued to look [not to violence but] to the next general election to restore his fortunes'.[9]

But this last type of political ambivalence, though striking because it involved, potentially, the lives and deaths of others and not merely, say, their levels of taxation, was fundamentally commonplace. It promised or threatened, but avoided commitment to a course. Far different was the ambivalence of the master-concept. Carved deep into the granite of the Parnell monument, which stands appropriately enough perhaps at the culmination of O'Connell Street in Dublin, are Parnell's best remembered words, 'No man has a right to set a boundary to the march of a nation'. But no carved words record that this characteristic sibylline threat–promise had been immediately preceded by a very specific limitation of Home Rule, for the present age, to the principles and system of 1782. A few moments earlier Parnell had asked for 'the restitution of that which was stolen from us towards the close of the last century'. 'We cannot', he went on,

> ask for less than restitution of Grattan's parliament, with its important privileges and wide and far-reaching constitution. We cannot under the British constitution ask for more than the restitution of Grattan's parliament.[10]

'Restitution' was the incantation of Home Rule. It was this very word which had opened the constitution of the Irish National League, the main Home Rule organisation. The first objective was declared to be 'the restitution to the Irish people of . . . a parliament elected by [themselves]'.[11]

Thus Home Rule, like repeal, used as its particular explanatory reference an apparently specific but essentially empty precedent. The Irish reverberations of '1782' were quite sufficient for the building of a popular front. The revolutionary potential in the idea of legislative independence was counteracted by the preservative concept of restoration; while the cruel reality of Irish sectarian hatred was masked by the association of Protestantism and patriotism implicit in the resurrection of Grattan. We might even add that all this constituted little more than a stalking-horse. The *fundamental* purposes – or at least functions – of Home Rule in Ireland were, under cover of a seeming political demand, to create or re-create national self-respect after two decades of humiliation and abasement, and to fuse the disparate elements of native power into a single aggressive unit.

The extraordinary success of the venture during 1879–82 so built up both the Irish party's leverage at Westminster, and Parnell's domination at home, that when Gladstone at last defined Home Rule in 1886 – naturally the first man to do so was a British politician – his interpretation could safely be adopted as also the Irish view. 'I am convinced', Parnell responded to Gladstone's outline of the Bill,

> that it will be cheerfully accepted by the Irish people and by their Representatives as a solution of the long-standing dispute between the two countries.[12]

In the debate Gladstone himself looked back to 1782. But not Parnell: the contrast between the vision of a dual monarchy of equal and equally autonomous nations, which that had been meant to convey, and the Dotheboys colonial assembly actually proposed in Gladstone's Bill was too painful to draw out. But, of course, the historical reality of 'Grattan's Parliament' had been a body ultimately controlled by London, and very largely composed of men with a heavy stake, ultimately speaking, in the maintenance of British supremacy. The current reality of Gladstone's counter-proposition was a *native* representative assembly, with a nationalist majority and no external manipulation. Naturally, with a local habitation and a name, Home Rule passed into an altogether different order of politics. It was now a lump of government putty, to be pummelled and kneaded, added to or torn from in committee. At the same time, we must not forget that it was the ambiguity which had produced the putty, in the end.

IV

Griffith's Sinn Fein can scarcely be described as a midnight performance of Parnell. For one thing, he was playwright rather than performer. He had neither the desire nor the disposition for political leadership. He did not even intend to form a party or to challenge or rival the Nationalists in the constituencies. Although a faithful Parnellite – and how strange the depth of fidelity which Parnell could command, especially from the grave – he was bitterly opposed from first to last to the two dominant traits of Parnellism, the cult of personality and the parliamentary method. How Griffith reconciled his adulation of Parnell with Sinn Fein's campaign against the Irish predilection for dictatorial 'chiefs' and the servile worship of power it is impossible to say. Perhaps a Dublin working-boy's hero worship simply lived on, secured like the fly in amber by Parnell's death. In after life, as Dr Richard Davis has pointed out, Griffith used to recall 'a handshake with Parnell on the way to the election meeting [at Creggs] where he caught the virus which killed him'.[13] Griffith did however attempt to justify or at least explain away the Westminsterism, despite the patent fact that Parnell owed both his standing and his achievement to his defiance and exploitation of the giants of the late-Victorian House of Commons. Griffith argued that Parnell's parliamentary participation was always contingent, that secession was the ultimate weapon which he would have used the moment he adjudged the parliamentary method to have run its course. He also argued that obstructionism was a form of the passive resistance to British claims to supremacy which was Sinn Fein's *raison d'être*. But if Griffith really believed either proposition, he must have either worked to deceive himself or else fallen a very easy victim to Parnell's accustomed sleight of hand.

The fact that Griffith wished to play the *éminence grise* and not the political warlord, and the fact that he eschewed a formal party, added if anything to the ambiguity of Sinn Fein. He was not opposed to the movement's having a clear leader or at least a 'monarch', if only he could find a Louis XIII whom he could serve as Father Joseph. In fact, the Hungarian analogy which Griffith cherished suggested that he should seek a Dēak. The most likely Dēaks among his gentry-supporters, John Sweetman and Sir Thomas Esmond, failed in the event to fill the role. But the search for such a figure drew Griffith himself slowly towards the right, as well as enlarging the *omnium gatherum* aspect of Sinn Fein. Similarly, the non-party or supra-party character, which down to 1917 Griffith strove not altogether successfully to maintain, tended inevitably towards ambiguity. This was partly because Griffith sought a common ground for Home Rulers and separatists, constitutionalists and republicans, even Irish-Irelanders and unionists. Such a degree of attempted comprehensiveness could not avoid variety of interpretation of key words and concepts. But the Griffith *modus operandi* worked in the same direction. In many ways, Griffith intended that Sinn Fein should perform in Ireland similar functions to those of the Fabian Society in Britain – that is, policy-formation through discussion, propaganda, the permeation of existing bodies and organisations, and political action at local level and on terms of an agreed 'non-party' programme. Again, this gave the movement a bias towards 'Broad-Churchism' and heterogeneity of meaning.

Deeper down, Griffith's images (he himself would have called them analogy, legality and historical truth) helped to broadcast useful illusions. The Hungarian policy, based on the applicability of the Austro-Hungarian *Ausgleich* of 1867 to Anglo-Irish circumstances, did provide a sort of metaphor for both parity and minimal conjunction between Great Britain and Ireland. In fact, fundamental differences between the two cases are readily apparent. The Hungarian revolution of 1848 would probably have succeeded had not another Great Power, Russia, intervened: there was nothing like a potentially successful revolution in Ireland in the nineteenth century. Similarly, the Austro-Hungarian accord had depended upon common internal enemies and victims, in particular the Slavs. There were no Irish Slavs – or British Slavs either, unless the Irish themselves might be crammed into such a role. Contrariwise, there was no Hungarian Ascendancy or Hungarian Ulster. None the less, even if the Hungarian example dissolved at the touch when regarded as a strict precedent, it still served well enough as a symbol of moderate Irish aspiration.

Constitutionalism was also well accommodated by an antiquarian juridical appeal. Griffith argued against the validity of the Act of Union on several grounds. First, the Renunciation Act of 1783, whereby Great Britain formally abandoned its claims to legislate for or influence the legislation of Ireland, had never been repealed. Secondly, the Act of Union was 'fraudulent' in that the Irish majority in its favour was achieved by bribery, in terms of money, honours or jobs. Finally, it was – again in Irish terms – *ultra vires*: the sovereign Parliament of Ireland had no constitutional power to resolve itself out of existence. Perhaps none of these grounds was really substantial in law. But none was without some shade of plausibility – and this was sufficient for Griffith's purpose. It gave colour to his claim that the unilateral establishment (or, as he would have put it, re-establishment) of an Irish House of Commons in Dublin was not a revolutionary step, but a return to legality. At the same time, the very phrase of 'the King, Lords and Commons of Ireland' was reassuring to Irish conservatives, whatever their party inclinations. In short, this entire line of argument represented an elaboration of the preservative or restorative element in the great nineteenth-century campaigns.

But the ambiguities in Sinn Fein went much deeper than Griffith's equivocal position within his own movement or the latitude permitted (or enjoined) by his political methodology. In the first place, it mapped the road only as far as a half-way house. The immediate programme was passive resistance to British rule in Ireland. This could appeal equally to parliamentarians despairing of Westminster, after a decade of Unionist ministries and Nationalist party disunion, and to Irish Republican Brotherhood (IRB) men who despaired of mounting a campaign of violence in the near or even medium future. Both categories were numerous by 1905. Moreover, the means proposed for resisting passively had also a multiple appeal. To withdraw the Irish members from Westminster so that they could set up, unilaterally, their own House of Commons in Dublin could be represented as either an arch-constitutional development or an anti-constitutional departure. Even short of this drastic step, the use of the Irish county councils to lay the foundations of autonomous government, and the 'Buy Irish' and similar little-Ireland campaigns, could be interpreted as either part of a process of breaking the connections with England, *à la* Tone, or else a simple expression of sturdy patriotism in which even an Irish Unionist, if public-spirited, might conscientiously participate. Underlying the whole was the hidden or half-hidden well of anglophobia on which all such moves could draw once they had achieved momentum. They thus represented a safe and comparatively inexpensive means of emotional indulgence, without commitment to either physical disturbance or particular goals. Sweet were the uses of ambiguity at this shallow level.

The fundamental dualism in Sinn Fein could not however be altogether contained, even in its most Fabian and powerless days. The objective of all the proposed passive resistance and the supersession (so far as might be) of the imperial order in Ireland was the demoralisation of the British government and the weakening of its will to dominate. But what was to follow? The moderates in Sinn Fein (and Griffith himself soon evolved into a, if not the leading, moderate) aimed at negotiation leading to settlement by compromise. The extremists however would regard British demoralisation as the signal for the opening of a violent campaign, doubtless a guerrilla war, to drive the enemy entirely out of Ireland, and establish an unfettered republic. This dualism was to become a critical factor in nationalist Ireland, in 1917–21. But well before it left the heights of theoretical disputation, it rendered Sinn Fein a Janus-faced body, with all the tensions, contrary impulses and internal struggles which such a collision of ends and of second-stage means necessarily implied.

The supreme form of Irish constitutional ambiguity, '1782' or 'Grattan's Parliament', played a larger role in Sinn Fein than in either the repeal or Home Rule movement. Griffith even used it as a touchstone for current tactical decisions. Thus, for example, Grattan's withdrawal from parliamentary engagement in the later 1790s was regarded by Griffith, in the context of a particular dispute of 1909, as a persuasive if not a binding precedent. There were several reasons for this extraordinary emphasis upon a stretch of comparatively remote and irrelevant history. First, as we have seen, 1782 might be taken to symbolise anything from a reassuringly conservative monarchical and oligarchic power structure at one end of the spectrum, to incipient separatism at the other. Secondly, 1782 had to be exalted if the arguments that the union was illegitimate and that the status quo ante was the moral reality were to be pressed home. But there were also special reasons why the 'age of Grattan' should appeal to Griffith. Grattan attracted him as an archetype of disinterested patriotism – and one from the other side of the Irish cultural divide, into the bargain. The benevolent paternalism which he discerned in the Irish Parliament of 1782–1800 was another attraction. Ironically enough for an apostle of self-rule, Griffith was more concerned with good government than with individual liberty of choice. Given Irishmen in command, he was decidedly of the 'whate'er is best administered is best' school of thought. Above all, Griffith saw the 'independence' of the late eighteenth century as essentially *economic* independence, for him the most critical form of national liberty. In his vision, Grattan's Parliament was the nursemaid – or even the mother – of Irish industry, and its supersession by Westminster the cause of Ireland's industrial and commercial decline. Thus in his version of Sinn Fein the magic year 1782 carried a much larger and more varied and particularised set of hopeful associations than it had ever done before; and since his reading of eighteenth-century history was both eclectic and tendentious the ambiguities of this emblem or symbol were proportionately multiplied.

One aspect of Dual Monarchy was never made explicit. The Crown had become for Irish Unionists of all types, and in particular northern Protestants, the outward and visible sign of the British connection – which was for them synonymous with security. The separate kingdom with the common king was thus, *inter alia*, a mode of squaring the circle of Irish fears and drives. Griffith had little or nothing to say directly upon the subject. He may well have felt that even the canvass of Protestant alarms at the prospect of a Catholic-dominated state would have soiled his faith in the supremacy of Irish nationality over all the divisive forces among the island's residents. He may even have felt, half-superstitiously, that silence would reduce if not dissipate the unpleasant reality. But his reactions to the Home Rule Bill of 1912 certainly showed his sensitivity to the Ulster part of the problem, as well as the great lengths he was prepared to go to allay Ulster feelings of insecurity. Not only was Ulster to be markedly overrepresented in the new Irish Parliament of his design, but its members were to be given a virtual veto and even quasi-autonomy on economic and industrial issues. Thus, the common Crown, though a routine consequence of employing the Austro-Hungarian model, may help to explain why that particular model was chosen. Without it, the latter-day Grattans and the Craigavons of the future could not possibly be drawn into an autonomous Irish state without conflict, not to say armed resistance.

V

Sinn Fein had then an almost Anglican comprehensiveness in terms of political utility. It could draw the violent and the pacific, the IRB man and the Nationalist, the Gaelic revivalist and the bicycle manufacturer, even the unionist and the republican, into some sort of association. Moreover, it could do so at a deeper level than that of ill-defined and open-sided formulae. It proclaimed a programme of significant, immediate action in which persons of all these types could join. Language and culture, home manufactures and local government, investment and education, could all be plausibly represented as spheres of potential cooperation in which a mutual Irish self-interest and identity could be expressed without necessarily abandoning one's inherited, traditional political commitment.

But of course Griffith himself had clear designs beyond this intermediate stage. More exactly, he had clear goals. The extent to which these goals would be achieved necessarily depended, even in his own prevision, upon the course of bargaining and the relative strength of the bargaining positions, when Britain was forced eventually into negotiations. None the less to a very remarkable degree the position which he sought was eventually realised in the Anglo-Irish agreement of December 1921, and its aftermath. The antitheses in early Sinn Fein and the projected sequences of events also proved curiously prophetic of the actual happenings of 1917–23.

Paradoxically, it was the armed rising of 1916 which gave Sinn Fein, as Griffith had originally visualised it, the vital opening. The movement had been effective in colouring 'advanced' Irish political thought, and in providing a sort of organisational and ideological staging post for people of various political inclinations. But Sinn Fein would probably have been accounted as of small importance, and Griffith himself have been adjudged an interesting curiosity, if not a mere vapouriser, had it not been for the Easter insurrection. Over the preceding century four major modes of applying Irish pressure upon Britain had been developed. The parliamentary party working directly upon the political system at Westminster had been pioneered by O'Connell and perfected by Parnell. Civil disobedience and passive resistance had really taken shape under Patrick Lalor's direction in the anti-tithe struggle of the 1830s, although of course O'Connell's massive campaigns of the 1820s and 1840s had practised it, obliquely, to some degree. O'Connell had also created – at least in the sense of articulating and advertising – the third form of pressure, the attempt to supersede parts of British government in Ireland by building up alternative native instruments of rule. His schemes for self-policing and indigenous legal arbitration, and his projected Council of Three Hundred (in effect a substitute for the House of Commons), had clearly pointed in this direction, even if it was not until the Land League's operations in the 1880s that a wholehearted attempt was made to put the technique into practice in a specific field. Finally, there was of course the direct challenge of the armed insurrection, the sacred sequence of 1798, 1803, 1848 and 1867, with each successive rebellion rendering the tradition more concentrated and inflexible.

The 1916 Rising represented, almost exclusively, the last and only the last of these four modes. That is to say, however intensive, it was also extremely narrow and wholly lacking in a further strategy. Yet, in experience, Irish pressure had always been most effective when several of its modes had been conjoined or even fused. The palmary instance was the Parnellite movement of 1880–6 when the first three were continually, though with varying emphasis, deployed, and even the spectre of the fourth was conjured up to hang like a checked *diabolus ex machina* over the scene. In contrast, the 'blood sacrifice' of 1916 represented a political cul-de-sac once it was over. On the other hand, the excitement and drama which it generated melted the moulds in which Irish mass-opinion had been fixed for more than a quarter of a century; and the ensuing plasticity provided Sinn Fein at last with its opportunity.

If then Sinn Fein was indebted to the militants for its chance to displace orthodox nationalism, the militants were no less dependent on Sinn Fein for capitalising upon their blow, in the immediate future. For Sinn Fein possessed both a strategy and a *modus operandi* where they were bankrupt. The general Sinn Fein emphasis on moral force and passive resistance, on mass-organisation and mass-pressure, were altogether pertinent in the aftermath of a demonstration of great earnestness and integrity by force of arms, and in the third disenchanted, conscription-threatening year of war. The radical, violent course needed the legitimation of popular sanction, if only retrospectively. In particular, endorsement at the polls was necessary if the Sinn Fein devices of tacit repudiation of British authority and the formation of alternative government were to carry weight. Still more, all these were necessary for Ireland to turn to account a new and apparently golden opportunity to win her independence – that is, by securing international recognition as an autonomous state in the course of the peace negotiations (conducted in a spirit of Wilsonianism) which would follow an Allied victory in the war.

Throughout 1917 the two movements, violent and pacific, converged and began to intertwine, first through the successful fighting of by-elections by militants wearing Sinn Fein colours and finally by a formal junction. At the Sinn Fein Ard-Fheis in December of that year, Griffith stood down from the presidency of his movement in favour of de Valera, who was already president of the Irish Volunteers. There was some piquancy in this particular arrangement. In form, de Valera's double presidency resembled Dual Monarchy, with the same person wearing both 'crowns' as the connecting link! But the dualism really went much deeper. In the concordat of December 1917, an independent Irish state – with a Provisional Government, a new citizenship and the promise of an indigenous administration – was assumed to have come into existence when it was proclaimed on Easter Monday 1916. Yet no actual attempt to operate such a state had been made or was as yet, apparently, intended. This would await international recognition. Hence a paradox: the assertion of the existence of an independent state was seen as a necessary preliminary to being represented as such at the negotiations; but it was to be the ratification of this independent state at the negotiations which would transform the claim into a reality! More paradoxical still, the recognition of the state internationally was to be the signal for the opening of negotiations with Great Britain to determine what sort of state it should be and what the constitutional relationship between the two islands – monarchy and republic, dual monarchy, commonwealth and dominion, or whatever – should become. At the same time, the military arm was suspended not abandoned. Thus, Sinn Fein in its new form maintained its original capacity to develop, or be developed, in various directions. But the Griffith version of the future – the assumption of self-government, British demoralisation and then the hammering out of something like Dual Monarchy at the bargaining table – was clearly in the ascendant once again.

Thanks primarily to the conscription issue – the British had their own ambiguities to pander to in April 1918! – the new post-1917 Sinn Fein secured the leadership of a national front and in due course the needed popular endorsement in the general election which followed immediately upon the Armistice. Then things went awry. True, Dail Eireann was set up, and the instruments of alternative government were projected. Moreover, Britain took no immediate suppressive steps lest the negotiations which it believed would have to come sooner or later might be imperilled. But on the very day that Dail Eireann (under the protection of the Dublin Metropolitan Police!) commenced its sitting, 21 January 1919, the opening shots of the Irish War of Liberation were fired, and the first Crown servants killed. This was symbolic of the dualism which was to reign in Ireland over the next thirty months. The constitutional method and the violent method were pursued simultaneously and apparently in harmony with each other. But it was violence, both in itself and in the British counter-violence which it inevitably provoked, which really dictated the course of events from mid-1919 onwards. Worst of all, in terms of Griffith's and de Valera's strategy, the attempt to secure international recognition of the Irish state at the peace negotiations failed utterly and instantly. The new Sinn Fein lost what was virtually its *raison d'être* overnight.

Yet *traditional* Sinn Fein was far from a spent force. In the first place, the strategy of passive resistance and the practical supersession of British authority in the Irish countryside probably contributed as much to the pressure upon Westminster and Whitehall as the guerrilla campaign itself. Secondly, whatever the die-hards and the inveterate gunmen might suppose, the essential point of the guerrilla campaign was to weaken the British will to continued domination, and to bring the British government to the bargaining table, desperate for a settlement. At this point, Griffithism must come into its own. So indeed it proved, quite literally. In de Valera's absence from – and despite Collins's presence in – the Irish delegation sent to London on 10 October 1921 to arrange a treaty, Griffith became the dominant Irish negotiator.

There is a real sense in which he was also the ultimate determiner of the Irish acceptance of the Treaty of 5–6 December. It was Griffith who secured Collins's agreement – could any other have done so? – and with this, the remaining members of the delegation fell domino-like into conformity. In a still more fundamental sense, the Treaty, from its Irish side, can be spoken of as Griffith's own. It embodied substantially his objectives and even more his attitudes of 1905 and later years. Dual Monarchy failed – by that name, at least. But the type of dominion status secured by the Treaty came close to this constitutional condition, in effect. Every other dominion was an area of comparatively recent white settlement; Ireland was a mother country. Every other dominion contained a very large population identifying itself, in spontaneous feeling, as British; truncated Ireland contained only a minute, despairing fragment of such people. In every other dominion, the oath of allegiance was simply to the Crown; in Ireland it was primarily to the state, and only secondarily to the king, as its titular head. Thus, the essential of Dual Monarchy as Griffith saw it, that is, separate states linked by a common nominal superior, was largely realised in the new Anglo-Irish arrangement. That was, as viewed from Dublin: the blessed ambiguity was of course that London could see it as an accommodation within a traditional and unbroken imperial structure. Moreover, with its one crucial symbol, the Crown, safely secured, London could ignore the fact that Ireland's new status was not stable, but would grow and develop unpredictably as the other dominions, and in particular the most radical, Canada, increased their measures of political independence. Again this was in keeping with the circumambience of traditional Sinn Fein. Griffith was certainly a believer in the march of nations; and it was Collins, under his influence, who claimed that the Treaty had won the freedom to win freedom.

All this was of course fatally limited by the fact that it applied not to the geographical entity, Ireland, but to only twenty-six of its thirty-two counties. Griffith himself must take much blame for the failure even to fight seriously or intelligently for the national integrity which Sinn Fein had always taken to be indispensable. Doubtless, the chances of success were always small. But his neglect to consider in time the issue of border arbitration is scarcely excusable. If not excusable, it is however, partly explicable by de Valera's obsession with engineering the 'break' – if the negotiations had to 'break' – upon the question of Ulster, rather than the Crown. This confused and divided the Irish delegation, to say the least.

De Valera was pursuing a different sort of ambiguity to Griffith's, for his eyes were turned inwards rather than outwards. De Valera's prime concern was to maintain the national front over which he had presided since 1917. Practically, this meant finding the minimum constitutional formulary and the minimum Irish political assertion which would be acceptable to the extreme separatists in his party. This he would then offer, as the utmost limit of Irish concession, to Great Britain – without perhaps any large hopes of its being accepted. *A fortiori*, de Valera's designs underestimated, if not wilfully ignored, the Ulster difficulty. But so far as the twenty-six redeemable counties were concerned, his was a farsighted venture. The formula of the 'external association' of a republic with the British empire was actually adopted in the case of India, with 'externality' on the one hand and 'association' on the other squaring the circle of republicanism and commonwealth. But the trouble with de Valera's legerdemain of 1921 was precisely that it was farsighted. It needed many developments and events of the next quarter-century to bring it within the range of the British possible – and even at that it could not help creating a problem of Irish irridentism in the 'lost' counties.

VI

Ambiguity in pacific politics was certainly related to the time scale, to demands being 'before their time'. Its great nineteenth-century expressions, repeal and Home Rule, were primarily directed at Great Britain. Their initial, domestic purpose was the mobilisation of a national movement by means of words, phrases and images which suggested parity and self-rule without any bloody or perilous severance. But the fundamental objective was to employ the pressure thus built up to force the British government to propose terms. Up to a point Griffith's Sinn Fein followed the same pattern, with Dual Monarchy acting in the role which repeal and Home Rule, in their turn, had already played. But it went further in two critical respects. First, self-government was not to await an Anglo-Irish settlement, but to be pressed forward, illegally but non-violently, to the utmost practicable degree: this would incidentally demoralise Westminster and predispose it to arrange an escape from Ireland. Secondly, Sinn Fein, as a loose movement rather than a drilled party, allowed for a variety of tactics and strategies beyond the generally agreed first stages, and it was quite as much concerned with its domestic as with its external effects. De Valera's formulae of 1921, 1933 and 1937 were traditional in allowing for a variety of meaning and interpretation. But they had moved on to new ground in at least three respects. They suggested, if they did not necessarily imply, a republic; they stressed the insurrectionary rather than the constitutional derivation; and their prime target was not British opinion but his old comrades in arms and their host of fellow travellers.

Even Griffith's original programme for a settlement was 'before its time'. Dual Monarchy was, as has been said, substantially the same as post-First World War dominion status. But it was far 'in advance' of dominion status as conceived of in 1905. The South African settlement of 1909 was to produce significant changes in that notion, and far more so the participation of the dominions in the First World War itself. De Valera's 'external association' of 1921, focusing on the Irish rather the British problem, was still more premature then than Griffith's concept had been in 1905. It required the experience of the Second World War, and to some extent the experience of that war's painful aftermath for all colonial powers, to reduce the British will to overseas domination to the point where such a view of a commonwealth could be endured. In a sense, then, all the major Irish constitutional ambiguities were prophetic, in terms of the limits of likely, or even conceivable, British concession at the time. Each sought to express today's outermost limits. But each succeeded in expressing only what would become practicable tomorrow. Cumulatively, however, they were effective. There is no road without an end, and the great *doubles entendres* served as so many Bailey bridges thrown across the chasms on the way.

Chapter 5

Politics Bellicose

I

Land and religion were for long the primary sources of violence in Ireland. For well over a century, the well-spring of armed force in politics was the agrarian secret society, and its later sectarian derivatives. As we have seen, their effectiveness depended upon threat and terror; these were ruthlessly employed as needed. The gun and knife, the instruments of maiming, killing and intimidation, were the means of enforcing a particular form of order upon the countryside. Moreover, the nature of the undertakings implied some rudimentary military characteristics, from the seizure and disposition of arms to the establishment of a hierarchy of decision and command.

Over predominantly Catholic Ireland, the relationship of, on the one hand, Whiteboyism, Ribbonism and their descendants and, on the other, the revolutionary (and even in some respects the constitutional) political movements of 1801–1922 was both intricate and ambivalent. They were at once alternatives and rivals. Sooner or later every constitutional party, from O'Connell's in the 1820s to Redmond's in the 1900s, condemned and dissociated itself from peasant law, as both disgraceful and diversionary. There were corresponding condemnations, for corresponding reasons, from every radical–revolutionary organisation, from the Young Ireland Left of the 1840s to the refurbished IRB of the present century. Yet, to a degree, the revolutionary parties were the heirs or beneficiaries of the Whiteboys; and much the same can be said of even the constitutional parties, in narrower form. It was the renewal of Whiteboyism in the early 1820s, upon a scale comparable with the 1780s, that rendered specific and terrible the unuttered threat of mass disorder to which Peel and Wellington surrendered, with Catholic Emancipation, in 1829. It was a further outburst of Whiteboyism which broke the tithe system in the next decade. It was the agrarian outrages of 1879–81 that gave Parnell the bricks for building. It was 'the last hurrah' of Whiteboyism in the west in 1898–9, which provided the driving force of a new mass agitation, that might well have regenerated the Irish Parliamentary Party, and reinvigorated the parliamentary method yet again.

Moreover, the strategy of all O'Connell's campaigns – and O'Connell's campaigns formed the model for subsequent 'constitutional' agitation in Ireland – was to intimidate by producing a vast (if possible, the illusion of a universal) combination in support of specific legislative objects. What was this but an expression, in daylight and upon a national scale, of what the Whiteboys had striven to effect, darkly and in localities, for more than half a century? Similarly, both the revolutionary United Irishmen of 1798 and the revolutionary Fenian movement of the early 1860s were sitting enthroned upon Whiteboyism in the countryside. It was critical in the growth of each to find a population habituated to conspiracy, to swearing in, to arms seizures and the rest. It was, to use a wry comparison, the counterpart of the priests taking over from the landlords, in the general election of 1826, the direction of 40s freeholders reared to vote *en bloc*. After all, the substitution was neither difficult nor unnatural. The republicans, in every generation, were aiming at a 'moral polity', the political equivalent, more or less, of the 'moral economy' of the peasants. Sinn Fein, as originally developed by Arthur Griffith, was the supreme expression of the 'moral polity' in that it aimed at the total supersession of official by native government; and the military methods of its instrument after 1917, the Irish Republican Army (IRA), were *mutatis mutandis* the military methods of 1761.

This is not to say that there is no fundamental distinction to be drawn between Whiteboyism and revolutionism, or between constitutional and violent politics. Nor is it to say that the leaders of either the parliamentary or the 'physical force' movements of 1800–1922 were disingenuous in distancing themselves from, and repudiating, agrarian terror and conspiracy. Nothing could be farther from the truth, in each particular case. We are always dealing with rival, hostile and competing forces. None the less it is undeniable that the violent, and even to a lesser extent the constitutional, parties were aided by, and to a degree dependent on, the traditional rural disorder and resistance. Thus the first paradox of 'politics bellicose' in Ireland is that its seed ground was petty, local, brutal *economic* conflict; and the second, that the national movements which this conflict fed, execrated it.

It is a third paradox that the agrarian secret society was generally conservative in tendency. As we have seen, it basically sought to preserve or restore what it conceived to be the ordained *equitable* relationships in the rural economy and community. This suggests the need for some modification of conventional Irish historiography. In this historiography, violence tends to be identified, simply and absolutely, with revolutionary politics. But in fact much of the agrarian violence which bred or supported political conspiracy was, literally speaking, reactionary in aim. Correspondingly, despite some apparent gropings by the Ribbonmen of the nineteenth century towards larger goals, the traditional secret society lacked national, let alone national–radical, objectives. Again, the received historiography needs an appropriate correction where it identifies physical force, in any automatic way, with republicanism or any other general revolutionary ideology.

II

If the secret society was the well-spring of violence in action in the nineteenth century, Wolfe Tone was – and is – the well-spring of violence in ideology from 1798 to the present day. Not for nothing has he been, and is he still, accepted as the Founding Father of the revolutionary nationalist tradition. There is some curiosity in this. He never fought and he despised all theorists. No blow, other than metaphorical, was ever struck by him for Irish liberty; he left no *Das Kapital* or *Mein Kampf* behind. He was moreover a comparative latecomer on the scene, and never high in the councils of the united Irishmen. None the less, it was his impress, rather than any other's, which was fixed upon Irish revolutionalism in its first modern form; and it was his particular traits and vicissitudes which worked their way into the nascent creed.

He began, as Dr T. J. Dunne has pointed out, as a marginal man in his society, 'the quintessential "outsider" – like Camus' hero, a colon alienated from colonial society, yet retaining its values and perspectives'.[1] As an Irish Anglican, born in 1761, he was privileged in numerous ways. But his lower-middle-class origins placed him at the start well outside the magic circle of the Ascendancy. He was however fortunate in possessing charm, talent and the patronage of the Wolfe family – and gaining in consequence a thorough education and a profession, law. This opened the way to, or rather raised the hope of entering the circle. The Ascendancy was itself a marginal class *vis-à-vis* Great Britain. One section found its satisfaction in serving British interests in Ireland, with the rewards of local power, office and status. But another section resented its inferiority and produced an Irish version of English Whiggery in response, stressing and seeking those constitutional, political and economic gains of 1688 which Englishmen were presumed to enjoy but the Anglo-Irish had still failed to secure. It was to this element in the Ascendancy that Tone adhered. As a faction it disappointed him: the opposition Whigs never provided him with the career or éclat he needed, although he did not despair of them finally until he was exiled from Ireland in 1795. But as a set of political ideas, Irish Whiggery served him throughout his life.

In the first place, he followed the Whigs in striving for a change of power-holders, although he saw the alternative government of Ireland in terms of a different class from them. They sought the replacement of pro-British Anglo-Irish hacks by independent-minded Anglo-Irish 'patriots', a change of men, not of ruling caste. Tone was however driven by his experiences to look outside the traditional Ascendancy altogether for his new rulers. It was on the mercantile and professional classes, and upon a junction of the educated Dissenters and Catholics, that he ultimately relied. But apart from the political changes and new social emphases consequential on such an alteration of the power-base, he went little further than the Whigs of the 1770s and 1780s. For him, the franchise was to be confined to £10 freeholders; the peasantry were to be 'paternalised' and gradually 'civilised' out of their barbarity; and generally the way was to be cleared for meritocracy and honesty in the public service. Careers open to talent and commerce open to enterprise represented the height of Tone's practical radicalism, which was indeed none too distant from the Manchester school of sixty years hence.

Again, he followed Whig lines in discerning in English rule, the fundamental source of Irish ills. The opposition Whigs had come to see Britain as the rock on which every effort at political reform perished. By this, they meant that the British administration in Dublin Castle and British influence over the Irish parliamentary representatives was normally powerful enough to keep their rivals secure in office and the system which frustrated them intact. Tone took this further than even the left-wing of the Ascendancy. In the end, he proposed absolute separation of two countries – 'breaking the connection' was literally intended – and not only did he come to regard England as the *sole* cause of Ireland's misgovernment, but also he hated her with the intensity of a personal vendetta. All this was certainly an 'advance' on Whiggery. But it was also an extension of the lines which the Whigs had drawn from the beginning. They had always, in true eighteenth-century fashion, looked to what might lever them into power. Obviously, the first step was to diminish English power in Ireland, for it was this above all which held them back. Naturally, they inclined towards political independence as a goal and anglophobia as an emotional indulgence. Tone may have writ much larger, but he was copying a familiar lesson.

This is no means to deny him originality. He carried the commonplace diagnosis of the Irish disease, as caused by the English connection, to the point of total repudiation of Britain and Empire; and this he rendered, not a dry conclusion, but a torrential passion. He carried the commonplace liberal aspiration for religious toleration and equality, both for their own sakes and as a means of defeating English designs, to the point of projecting a Dissenter–Catholic power alliance as the only guarantee of national separation and of an end to faction and corruption. He brought a new clarity to old arguments; he drove them forward logically; and he conjoined them effectively. This was certainly ideological novelty, however worn the materials with which he worked.

The other elements in the new creed were derived from his own character and contemporary circumstances rather than Whig tradition. First, he was a militarist and authoritarian by inclination. Soldiering attracted him from the start. His first scheme for fame and fortune was based upon a military colony in the Sandwich Islands, and his last role, to which he clung desperately to the end, was that of adjutant in the Army of the French Republic. In between, he was forever fascinated by uniforms, flags, weapons and battle; and he regarded armies, at any rate armies such as that of contemporary France and the hoped-for Army of

Ireland, as not merely the nation in arms, but almost as the nation *sans phrase*, and the repository of civic virtue and authority as well as force.

Tone also admired the element of order and discipline imposed from above in the French Republic. Liberty of expression and a free press were to be qualified by patriotic needs: there would be no free speech for traitors in Tone's Ireland. This was of course partly derived from the revolutionary's belief, which Jacobinism epitomised, that the party or group to which he belonged was the true representation of the people's will, and as such justified and indeed obliged to govern autocratically for the general good. Another novel element in Tone's creed, republicanism, may well have been fortuitous. In the late eighteenth century, the word carried none of the mystic overtones which it came to bear in Ireland in later years. It was simply the common contemporary name for non-monarchical government, a matter of business-like nomenclature rather than a Holy Grail. The fateful word 'republic' was possibly another chance acquisition of the times in which Tone lived.

Thus revolutionary nationalism as shaped ideologically by Tone was coloured by several accidents of his own career, era and disposition. By the same token, it was almost empty of positive content. Breaking the connection with England, and the eradication of English influence in Ireland, were the obsessive concerns. What would succeed independence was hazy indeed, especially in social and economic terms. Much rested, moreover, on the airy assumptions that religious antagonism among Irishmen was artificial, and that once recognised for what it really was – an overlord's device for dividing and conquering – it would cease to act as a barrier to national union.

It followed that there would be tensions and crosspurposes between extremist theory and Irish reality. The very rising of 1798 presaged the future discordances. The so-called 'United Irish' rebellion in Wexford was essentially sectarian and economic in motivation, and directed against Irish Protestants and Irish landed proprietors rather than Britain. This epitomised the contradiction between the ideal and the actual in violent resistance or counter-action for the next half-century. The vengeance of the agrarian secret society; the bloodshed which followed even open and constitutional campaigns such as the anti-tithe agitation; the disorders springing from religious aggression, or demonstrations of supremacy, by Irish Protestants – it was these which constituted the real 'physical force' in Irish politics before the great famine. They were repudiated as shameful, vicious and anachronistic by those in the revolutionary tradition; and such people laid the blame for them ultimately at Britain's door. Yet, Emmet's street brawl apart, such outbursts remained the only 'assertions' of anything in arms in Ireland from 1798 to 1848. Actual violence and Toneite theory were in fact antagonistic, the actual violence being directed at establishing that Protestant, Catholic and Dissenter *were* the real enemies of one another – to say nothing of

Landlord, Tenant and Labourer being in the same blood-ridden boat. This was the fundamental contradiction at the heart of the 'physical force' doctrine in the first half of the nineteenth century.

III

The revival of revolutionist nationalism in the later 1840s had little immediate connection with the United Irish tradition. It was a gradual development, or confluence of several developments, rather than a simple resurrection. Three factors seem to have been especially potent. First, from its beginning in 1842 the Young Ireland newspaper, the *Nation*, listed towards the side of arms. This was only to be expected. It was the mouthpiece of Davisism and therefore of romantic nationalism of the German, and more specifically the Prussian, type. The consequent emphasis upon national history and national glory was, inevitably, militaristic.

This implicit challenge to the pacific and constitutional methods of agitation currently enjoined by O'Connell upon the repeal movement was far from clear initially. Even O'Connell himself might have safely and happily endorsed the *Nation*'s favourite Irish feats of arms – those against the Tudor forces of the sixteenth century, the Parliamentary, Cromwelliam and Williamite armies of the seventeenth and (as the Irish Brigade) the anti-French coalitions of 1700–50. These were all, in rosy retrospect, chivalrous and heroic ventures; they were also usefully remote in time. Moreover they were generally celebrated in ballad verse. Whether rationally or not, this gave a sort of licence to martial and racial boastings and swathed the sword in the gauze of high-flown rhetoric and bombast. Typical of the genre was *The Ballad of Athlone*, glorifying a piece of Jacobite heroism of 1691, which opened:

> Does any man dream that a Gael can fear? –
> Of a thousand deeds let him learn but one![2]

Now in one sense this sort of thing was commonplace enough. Instances of British derring-do were trumpeted or memorialised by thousands of similar effusions in England in the nineteenth century – though it was not without significance that the *Nation* form always implied that Ireland was a sovereign power and thus indirectly asserted parity. But the *Nation* verse was also generally, if not invariably, anglophobic. The 'baseness' and 'treachery' of the 'Saxon' were favourite themes. Davis's *Lament for the Death of Eoghan Ruadh O'Neill* exemplifies the strain.

> 'Did they dare, did they dare, to slay Eoghan Ruadh O'Neill?'
> 'Yes, they slew with poison him they feared to meet with steel.'

'May God wither up their hearts! May their blood cease to flow!
'May they walk in living death who poisoned Eoghan Ruadh!

'Though it break my heart to hear, say again the bitter words.'
'From Derry, against Cromwell, he marched to measure swords:
But the weapon of the Sacsanach met him on his way,
And he died at Cloch Uachtar, upon St Leonard's day.'

More important still, the constant 'flash of pike and sword' [3] in the Young Ireland ballads — not to add the fact that they were composed as 'marching songs' – inevitably instilled militarism, especially in school-boy and adolescent breasts. Nor can there be much doubt that it was meant to do so, albeit for a vague future rather than immediate action. Davis himself wrote,

> The tribune's voice, and poet's pen
> May sow the seed in prostrate men;
> But 'tis the soldier's sword alone
> Can reap the harvest when 'tis grown.

The cumulative effect of years of such indoctrination was to change the disposition of large numbers in the coming generation. John O'Leary later recalled the *Nation*'s impact upon the schoolboys of the mid-1840s:

> In leading article, essay, and poem we read, from week to week, the story of Ireland's sufferings under English rule; and now and then we heard of other countries groaning under alien domination, and of their efforts, successful or unsuccessful, to shake it off. At first, perhaps, the teaching of the *Nation* was not directly unconstitutional, though, indirectly, it certainly was so from the beginning. From ceasing to 'fear to speak of '98' to wishing to imitate the men of that time the transition was very easy indeed to the youthful mind. Many, if not most, of the younger amongst us were Mitchelites before Mitchel, or rather before Mitchel had put forth his programme.[4]

In general, we can say that the common banality of the Young Ireland art, and its braggadocio and absurd inflation of sentiment (which Yeats was later to scarify), were no barriers to its influence in Ireland – any more than they would have been in any other European country in the 1840s. Posturing romanticism was the mode, and swift the spread of popular audiences in the hitherto non-reading classes.

The second reason for the revival of the cause of violence was simply that O'Connell's parade of pacifism and loyalty to the Crown in his repeal campaign, coupled with the campaign's failure in 1843, provoked a reaction in time. Flunkeyism and servility were unavoidable notes of the incessant expressions of devotion to the Queen which characterised the 'Loyal' Association. The harp was surmounted by the Crown on the repeal button, and even the membership card was boldly superscribed,

'God save the Queen'. Up to a point, the rank and file of the Association
could stomach all this as a tactical necessity and partial insurance against
suppression. But gradually and cumulatively it nauseated; and after the
proclamation of the mass meeting at Clontarf in October 1843, and still
more once the euphoria following O'Connell's acquittal in the subsequent state trials had evaporated, it seemed ever more evident that
pacificism and loyalty were prices being paid for nothing. At any rate,
they would not buy the goods which were being sought.

From 1845 on, the revulsion against meekness and submission grew,
with a corresponding increase in the feeling that political 'virility' needed
to be attested. Indeed, the assertion of such a virility had always been a
leitmotiv of O'Connell's own agitation. In particular, he had systematically used the image or analogy of slavery to rouse the masses to an
understanding of their condition. Byron's

> Hereditary bondsmen, know you not –
> Who would be free themselves must strike the blow?

was declaimed by him in innumerable speeches; and his celebrated
'defiance' at Mallow on 11 June 1843 began

> Are we to be called slaves? Have we not the ordinary courage of
> Englishmen? Are we to be trampled on? . . . it will be my dead body
> they will trample on, not the living man.[5]

Even O'Connell, then – at the very climax of his popular power –
half-proclaimed the indispensability of manhood and resistance. Can it
be any surprise that, among his followers, this feeling broke through
prudential restraints more and more frequently as he became politically
and physically enfeebled?

Ironically, it was O'Connell himself who sealed the identifications of
pacific politics with pusillanimity and bellicose with manliness. By mid-
1846 he had been much provoked by the Young Ireland faction in the
Association. He was moreover set upon a renewal of the Whig alliance,
and Lord John Russell had made it clear the Liberals regarded the Young
Irelanders as republican, separatist and revolutionary in inclination.
O'Connell's choice of battleground was pacifism, in, so to say, its most
violent form. He insisted that a pledge repudiating the use of physical
force in any circumstances be adopted by every member of the Association. This opened the way for – if not absolutely invited – T. F.
Meagher's celebrated oratorical flight when the resolutions came up for
determination at Conciliation Hall on 27 July.

> Be it for the defence, or be it for the assertion of a nation's liberty, I
> look upon the sword as a sacred weapon. And if, my lord, it has

sometimes reddened the shroud of the oppressor like the anointed rod of the high priest, it has at other times blossomed into flowers to deck the freeman's brow. Abhor the sword and stigmatise the sword? No, no, my lord, for in the cragged passes of the Tyrol it cut in pieces the banner of the Bavarian, and won an immortality for the peasant of Innspruck [sic]. Abhor the sword and stigmatise the sword? No, no my lord, for at its blow a giant nation sprang from the waters of the Atlantic, and by its redeeming magic the fettered Colony became a daring free Republic. Abhor the sword and stigmatise the sword? No, my lord, for it scoured the Dutch marauders out of the fine old towns of Belgium, back into their own phlegmatic swamps, and knocked their flag, and laws, and sceptre, and bayonets into the sluggish waters of the Scheldt.[6]

Although O'Connell carried the day and remained till he died secure in mass support, it was a pyrrhic victory. Meagher's instances of armed force overthrowing foreign 'tyranny' and establishing 'national' independence were all familiar and revered cases in repeal propaganda; and over and above the particular examples, the issue which had been forced upon the Association could not but polarise eventually, in the popular mind, into a choice between cravenness and courage. For a tactical advantage, O'Connell had sold a good deal of future. Political virility had been, to a dangerous degree, identified with violence.

Thirdly, for all the vapourising and poetastering in the *Nation* school, it was bound sooner or later to attract activists to its ranks. John Mitchel's succession to Davis as editor of the newspaper in the autumn of 1845 marked, in all respects, a change in emphasis. In November of that year, writing upon the implications for insurrection of the coming of the railways to Ireland, Mitchel stressed their vulnerability to sabotage and ambush. The repeal wardens, he added, should be trained 'in the military uses and abuses of railways'.[7] This was a practically open anticipation of guerrilla war, and one moreover which actually envisaged the officers of O'Connell's Association as participants. Of course, one can vapourise in prose about future 'dirty' war as well as in verse about past chivalry and valour; and Mitchel himself was certainly no Garibaldi. None the less the discussion of immediate and practical insurrectionary tactics represented a critical change. The first turning towards actual violence had been taken. The inexperienced fumbling of the embryonic revolutionists in 1846–7, and the opera bouffe character of the few Irish revolutionary events of 1848, must not mislead us. Sooner or later, serious and capable militists were bound to emerge, once physical force doctrines had taken a grip upon a considerable body of the younger men. After all, the February Revolution of 1848 in Paris itself was a theatrical and a theoreticians' affair rather than a 'professional' conflict. But it was soon to be succeeded, in the form of the July Revolution, by an organised, purposive and sanguinary uprising. Similarly, in Ireland itself there was a handful of men who attempted to open a genuine guerrilla campaign in late 1848 and early 1849. Thus, it seems a fair conclusion that revolutionism gradually revived in Ireland over the years 1842–8 because of three convergent developments – the glorification of 'historic' violence, growing shame at subservience and appeasement, and the inevitable entry of the gun upon such a scene.

IV

Failure and famine scattered many of the proto-revolutionaries of the late 1840s both east and west, in particular to France and the United States. In each place, their ideas were coloured and developed by local circumstances. The eventual junction of the two separate streams had to wait practically a decade, until 1858. When it came, 'Fenianism' (to use an imprecise but indispensable term) was the result.

Dominant in the French strain was James Stephens, who had sought refuge in Paris in 1848 after his escape from Ireland. Stephens was a classical nineteenth-century revolutionary conspirator, indomitable, unshakeable in his faith in ultimate success, visionary, tyrannical, vain, suspicious and both single- and closed-minded. He was not the man to acknowledge indebtedness to others. But in two respects his later ideology matched contemporary Parisian modes so closely that it seems reasonable to infer some measure of derivation. First, the Paris of the Second Republic was the international capital of insurrectionists, many of them the debris of the failed European revolutions of 1848–9. Here conspiracy of the Carbonarist type regrouped, and absorbed the lessons of defeat. In this milieu, Stephens could well have found his particular version of the secret oath-bound society dedicated to the overthrow of established government. It was a highly schematised form of organisation, minimising the dangers of official penetration and of the informer in its ranks, and maximising central direction. By Stephens's scheme, the movement was divided into 'circles', the equivalent of military regiments. Each 'circle' was commanded by a 'centre', A, who chose nine Bs (or junior officers), who in turn each chose nine Cs (or NCOs), who in turn each chose nine Ds (or rank and file). A 'centre' was to be known only to his Bs, and a B only to his Cs, and a C only to his Ds. Correspondingly, the 'head centre' (Stephens himself, of course) was to be known only to his immediate subordinates; and the orders of each officer were absolutely binding upon the rank immediately below. Authority flowed from the top, obedience mounted step by step from below; and the secrecy enjoined on all was to be double-guarded by the comparatively minor consequences of any particular failure in the chain.

Stephens's second possible Parisian debt may have been to neo-Jacobinism, in particular to the version expounded by Blanqui in 1848 and later years. Blanqui, an extreme republican in the revolutionary tradition, eschewed social and economic objectives, at any rate immediately, and concentrated upon the actual seizure of power and the overthrow of 'illegitimate' government. The Blanqui-ists saw themselves as acting for 'the People'. No matter if they were in a popular minority: this merely meant the postponement of elections until the 'mission of democratic enlightenment' had changed sufficient minds. Force to grasp political control, and dictatorship (for as long as might be necessary) to hold it, were Blanqui's principles of action. Stephens left no political testament, but his own conduct and the stamp which he impressed upon the later Irish revolutionary movement were redolent of this creed and programme.

The other stream of Fenianism, the American, was certainly ambiguous in its early stages of development. It originated in the New York Emmet Monument Committee of late 1853. The name suggests that most unlikely thing, a revolutionists' pun or joke. Clearly it referred to Emmet's speech from the dock eschewing an epitaph for himself until Ireland had taken her place among the nations of the earth. This was in itself amorphous. Ireland could be regarded as a 'nation' and yet stand in various constitutional relationships to Great Britain. The reason for the committee's formation, however, implied a specific link with the United Irishmen and the doctrine of 'England's difficulty, Ireland's opportunity'. With the outbreak of the Crimean War, Nicholas I's Russia became the (somewhat strange) surrogate for Revolutionary France. In fact, the Russian 'alliance' never materialised. None the less the arrival of a new factor in Anglo-Irish conflict had been signalled. This was the formation, through massive emigration, of an Irish-American community, considerable numbers of whom were bitterly anglophobic. To these people, the United States appeared both as a secure base in which to plan revolutionary action and as an international power, potentially hostile to Britain, which might be induced to use its influence to reduce or remove British oppression in Ireland.

The New York committee of 1853 quickly adopted the expedient of forming military companies of Irish Americans, or more exactly of using existing companies for Irish revolutionary purposes. The companies were seen as the expeditionary army of the future. Yet, currently, they were encorped in the New York state militia as regular regiments of volunteers. Thus from the start ambivalence lay at the heart of the Irish-American radicalism. This was to become both overt and acute by the 1860s.

The question was, would Irish nationalist activities involve the United States in the dreaded 'foreign entanglements'? The native reaction, at its most moderate, was expressed by the Chief Justice of the United States Supreme Court in passing judgement on naturalised Irishmen who had formed a revolutionary club in Cincinnati:

> I censure no Irishman for sympathizing with his native land [but] these feelings ought not to be indulged in at the hazard of the interests and peace of the country of his adoption. . . . The obligations of citizenship cannot exist in favor of different nationalities at the same time.[8]

But commitment to two different nationalities at the same time was precisely what Irish-Americans commonly aspired to. It was natural, if also self-contradictory, for them to seek to identify themselves with, as well as to distinguish themselves from, the main body of Americans. Such ambivalence is commonplace among immigrant groups and readily comprehensible in terms of striving for equality of status. To put the matter generally: Irish-Americans in the third quarter of the nineteenth century found themselves *en masse* in a situation of economic, social, and in certain senses even civic inferiority. Their collective response was to use their numbers and their local concentration against the established classes. But they were caught between two magnets: their solidarity as a distinctive group and their passion for acceptance as equals, or even as one of the master races, in American society at large.

In all this, Irish-American nationalism at once expressed defiance of the American social hierarchy *and* was looked to as a means of winning social acceptance in America. If (the Irish-American argument would have run) the Irish were victims of the same imperial system that had debased the thirteen colonies in the eighteenth century; if they were engaged in the continuation of the very struggle from which the United States had been born – then were they not on a level, in aspiration and civic virtue, with the rest? 'Dual allegiance' had, therefore, an interior dualism of its own. Of course, Irish-American nationalism was critically important in later Irish politics. But it was also an American phenomenon, developed by and among Americans, and with American ends in view. To a degree this applied even to Fenianism. We should not forget that the very words 'Revolutionary' and later 'Republican', used successively to describe the Brotherhood signified by IRB, were by no means radical but rather hallowed and highly respectable appellations of historic associations in the United States.

Thus, the American strain of Irish revolutionism in the 1850s was inward as well as outward looking. It was concerned with the mustering and deployment of both anglophobic sentiment in the United States and arms and money; it was eager for violent action in Ireland and much inclined to images of forces setting sail to land in and liberate the homeland. All this meant an extraordinary degree of 'open' activity, even a quest for publicity, on the part of the clandestine organisation. John O'Leary was amazed, when he reached New York in 1859 as the covert agent of the IRB, to find himself 'serenaded' in public by the brass band of the celebrated '69th New York'; called on to address the crowd of 'conspirators' in the street from the window of his hotel; replied to by the

Fenian leader, 'Colonel' Michael Doheny, in the worst strains of mob oratory; and finally having his 'mission' reported in the columns of one of the Irish-American journals. It was, as O'Leary said, 'a queer sort of proceeding to give a public, or semi-public, reception to a secret envoy';[9] but it was also inherent in the nature of the Irish-American movement.

To a marked degree, the IRB, formally established on St Patrick's Day 1858, represented an amalgam of the French and American varieties. The oath administered to the first members ran:

> I, A. B., in the presence of the Almighty God, do solemnly swear allegiance to the Irish Republic, now virtually established, and that I will do my very utmost, at every risk, while life lasts, to defend its independence and integrity; and, finally, that I will yield implicit obedience in all things, not contrary to the laws of God, to the commands of my superior officers. So help me God. Amen.[10]

In this there are some interesting curiosities. What is the meaning, and what the implication, of '*virtually* established', or of '*defend* its independence', or of '*integrity*'? Why, and to what effect, qualify the swearing of absolute obedience to superior officers with 'not contrary to the laws of God'? But perhaps the most striking feature of the oath is its absorption with the deed, to the exclusion of all consideration of the consequences. The nature of Irish society, of the Irish economy and of religion in the new order were not only ignored, but also forbidden (because potentially divisive or distracting) questions. Even the avowed existence of an 'Irish Republic' may have implied nothing about the form of government once the 'state' passed from the metaphysical into the physical order. O'Leary, 'the only [Fenian] who has said or written anything to the point',[11] contemplated even Dual Monarchy with equanimity.

> Let England cease to govern Ireland, and then I shall swear to be true to Ireland and the Queen or King of Ireland, even though that Queen or King should also happen to be Queen or King of England. It is not, nor has it ever been with me, any question of forms of government, but simply of freedom from foreign control.[12]

In one sense, this last was the key to Fenianism. Its universal, overriding objective, what all Fenians had as their common aim, was, simply, the eradication of British influence in Ireland. As O'Leary himself concluded, 'English rule, directly or indirectly, proximately or remotely, [was] at the bottom of the whole trouble . . . and to shake, if not to shatter, that rule, was then, and is still, the great aim, or, if you will, dream of my life'.[13]

Thus, Fenianism's prime contribution to the armoury of violence was not ideological, but a revolutionary methodology. True, the methodology included the immediate assumption of national authority – a later form of the Fenian oath identified, as interchangeable, 'the Supreme Council of the Irish Republican Brotherhood and the Government of the Irish Republic' – and this had important psychological as well as practical implications. As Kolakowski describes the resultant Utopian mentality,

> Believing in a higher-order reality that is set into the present and, though undiscernible to the naked eye, is the genuine reality justifies the utter contempt for actually existing people who scarcely deserve attention when contrasted with the seemingly non-existent, but much more important generations of the future.

But the core of the Fenian methodology was the ultimate resort to armed force, and the steps preparatory to the denouement. In part, such steps were conspiratorial after the Carbonari model; and these were to reach their apotheosis in the prelude to the Easter Rising of 1916 when the innermost circle of the IRB systematically deceived even its own president – to say nothing of its allies or its rank and file. Well before 1916, however, the conspiratorial method was extended from the actual military organisation of the movement to the use of 'front' associations and the infiltration, manipulation and, if possible, control of useful bodies. The Gaelic Athletic Association and the Gaelic League are leading instances. All this may plausibly be represented as French-derived.

But revolutionary preparation also drew upon the American strain, in particular, for the provision of a sea in which insurrectionary fish might not only swim but also be spawned. Here the decisive precedent was the funeral of Terence Bellew McManus in 1861. McManus, a minor Young Irelander sentenced to transportation in 1848, had escaped from Van Diemen's Land in 1851 and settled in San Francisco where he conducted a rather unsuccessful business and led a rather unsteady life until his death ten years later. Upon his death, indeed some time after his first burial, a group of local Fenians conceived the notion of a great demonstrative journey for his remains, 6,000 miles to Glasnevin cemetery in Dublin. The scheme was taken up by the New York and other American Fenians. True to the spirit of clandestinism, Stephens and his coterie in Dublin initially disapproved. But when it became clear that the project could not be aborted, they devoted themselves to controlling things in Ireland, to maximising the scale and dramatic impact of the processions, and to turning the affair into a show of strength for the Fenian *as against* every other form of Irish nationalism.

The venture succeeded beyond the expectations of the most sanguine. From the day that McManus's body left San Francisco, 2 August 1861, until the day of the Irish reburial, 10 November, it served its intended purpose. Apart from the demonstrations it evoked in the United States, particularly New York, it produced massive shows of sympathetic strength (readily appropriated by the Fenians) in Cork, at Tipperary Junction and finally at the lying-in-state in the Dublin Mechanics Insti-

tute – Archbishop Cullen had prohibited the use of any city church for
the purpose – and the great funeral march to Glasnevin. The Dublin
cortège exceeded 50,000 in number and marched 7 miles through
crowded streets. The Fenians had reason for their 'posthumous' exul-
tation. They had assembled and disciplined vast numbers. They had
successfully defied clerical condemnation. They had, though probably a
minority, dominated the Irish organising committees. They had beaten
off their Young Ireland and other nationalist rivals for control of
McManus's body. Finally, they had wrestled successfully for the right to
deliver the funeral oration. Though the speech was read by 'Captain'
Smith of San Francisco, the composition was Stephens's, who thus
served as the pioneer of this particular variety of perfervid exhortation
and prophetic utterance. In short, the Fenians had hit upon the means of
tapping and canalising the wild waters of indeterminate anglophobic
sentiment in their fellow-countrymen. They had discovered that death
and martyrdom could be enlisted in their ranks. It was the beginning of
the long line of potent shades and calculated rhetoric with which we are
so familiar.

V

Pearse's father was an archetypal English Victorian radical: artisan-
craftsman, autodidact, Bradlaughlite-atheist (initially), William
Morrisite, and sturdy and pugnacious individualist. Pearse himself
occasionally worried lest his parentage had left him socially schizophrenic, with the cold, repellent, humourless English side in battle with
Gaelic joyousness and fire. Although, in general, his paternity seems
at odds with his career, a few elements seem to match, to a degree.
Obviously, there is a case for regarding Pearse's extreme Gaelophilia as a
compensation for his imperfect Irish identification, though this would be
mere inference from his general circumstances: there appears to be no
other evidence in support. We can perhaps see reflections of the elder
Pearse in the younger's earnestness, didacticism and obsessions, and in
some other of the marks of the enthusiast; and they were at one in
enjoying the artistic impulse. But perhaps the most curious of all the
possible derivations from his father was Patrick Pearse's largeness of
mind and toleration of opposing opinion. These are extraordinary qualities in a zealot. But, at any rate until, in his final years, he was drilled into
the hatred of both enemies and heterodoxy which went with commitment to the IRB, Pearse truly was a magnanimous fanatic. He was
prepared to accept half-measures such as the Irish Councils Bill of 1907
in the hope of building on, and turning to account, such mild concessions
as they offered. He willingly learnt, and was eager to make the *amende
honorable* as his views enlarged: the change-about in his attitude to Yeats
and the Literary Revival is a case in point. He was never personally

rancorous: in the last throes of the Easter Rising, he took steps to safeguard Eoin MacNeill's reputation, although MacNeill had, albeit conscientiously, damaged the cause severely.

But Pearse was more the 'child' of his times than of his father. His adolescence in the 1890s coincided with widespread revulsion from constitutional politics in favour of cultural separatism. For twenty years, from 1893 to 1913, Pearse's guiding star was the Gaelic language, and the values and life-form which this was taken to embody. In fact, it was only ten months before his death that he delivered, in a graveside panegyric of the Fenian, O'Donovan Rossa, his fateful incantation, 'not free merely, but Gaelic as well; not Gaelic merely, but free as well' – thus suggesting not merely an interconnection, but even absolute parity in importance, between revolutionary and cultural nationalism. This probably misrepresented the balance in Pearse's own mind at so late a date. By July 1915 revolutionary nationalism had, for him, replaced cultural nationalism as the predominating need. None the less, his welding of the two, in his final rhetoric and writing and in particular in his memorable graveside phrases, was to have a profound effect on later Irish history. He had identified a Gaelic-speaking Ireland with the politics of violence. The 1916 Rising was to sanctify and cement the junction.

Secondly, Pearse strongly reflected his age in his emphasis upon blood, force and youth. Early-twentieth-century Europe, which had known no protracted war of considerable scale for almost one hundred years, contained many 'romantics' more than half in love with 'clean', violent death and the expenditure of young lives for great causes. No one exceeded the Pearse of 1913–15 in (what must seem to us) perverted 'nobility'.

> I am glad that the Orangemen have armed [in 1913], for it is a goodly thing to see arms in Irish hands. . . . We must accustom ourselves to the thought of arms, to the sight of arms, to the use of arms. We may make mistakes in the beginning and shoot the wrong people; but bloodshed is a cleansing and a sanctifying thing, and the nation which regards it as the final horror has lost its manhood.[14]

Or, apropos of the war in 1915,

> It is good for the world that such things should be done. The old heart of the earth needed to be warmed with the red wine of the battle-fields. Such august homage was never before offered to God as this, the homage of millions of lives given gladly for love of country.[15]

Again, the prize offered by Pearse in 1914 to the boys at his school, St Enda's, for 'a genuine effort to speak Irish' was – a rifle! While it is only fair to remind ourselves of Pearse's happy inexperience of violence – he may never have heard a shot fired to maim, or seen a gun wound or a killed human, before Easter Monday 1916 – we must also attribute to him much of the romanticisation of bloody death, almost as its own end, in later Irish revolutionism.

Pearse was moreover idiosyncratic in conceiving all this in Christian, and, specifically, Catholic terms. It is not hyperbole to speak of Pearse's *religion* of nationalism. This was simple truth in three senses. First, he cast himself – and other nationalists – in various biblical roles, as witness-martyr, as scapegoat, as suffering servant, as redeemer. Even in boyhood Pearse's 'greatest devotional zeal was reserved for the Holy Week ceremonies and the crucified Christ'.[16] This most uncommon choice of Catholic devotional emphasis remained with him to the end. Translated into revolutionary terms, it served to produce the very unusual ideals of passivity (in the literal sense that suffering things to be done to one is more significant than what one does oneself) and of bearing testimony, even at the ultimate price, the laying down of life. Secondly, Pearse assumed, in a quite unqualified fashion, that Ireland's cause was, and had always been, a holy war. 'In the battle order, God was ranged upon [the Gael's] side, the side fighting for Our Savior's faith against the Gall'[17] – or foreigner or invader. Finally, he merged orthodox Catholicism and Irish insurrectionism to form virtually a new faith. The translations from orthodox religion were pedantically exact: parody might even be inferred were the author any other than Pearse himself. The Irish people was he wrote, like the Christian soul, made in God's image and likeness; Irish nationality too had its four evangels – Tone, Davis, Mitchel and Lalor; national freedom bore the same four marks as divine religion, in its unity, sanctity, catholicity and apostolic succession.

> Of unity, for it contemplates the nation as one; of sanctity for it is holy in itself and in those who serve it; of catholicity, for it embraces all the men and women of the nation; of apostolic succession for it, or the aspiration after it, passes down from generation to generation from the nation's fathers.[18]

Nor was it only a matter of transposition. The two creeds actually joined. Pearse's Mionn (or Oath) of 1912 is a fair instance:

> In the name of God,
> By Christ His only Son,
> By Mary His gentle Mother,
> By Patrick the Apostle of the Irish,
> By the loyalty of Colm Cille,
> By the glory of our race,
> By the blood of our ancestors,
> By the murder of Red Hugh,
> By the sad death of Hugh O'Neill,

> By the tragic death of Owen Roe,
> By the dying wish of Sarsfield,
> By the anguished sigh of Fitzgerald,
> By the bloody wounds of Tone . . .[19]

Pearse's last contribution to the repertoire of violent politics was, literally speaking, dramatic. He really did see rebellion as a drama. It was – or should be – the re-enactment of a classical tragedy by each generation, successively. It was meaningful as a heroic gesture rather than as an effective act. It embodied roles to play.

Pearse's own role in the Easter Rising was double-natured. First, the rising represented the climax of a sacrifical life. Once the battle began, however, Pearse had no function to perform in the General Post Office other than the rhetorical. From Easter Monday onwards he was, in effect, a Shakespearean hero who had received his fatal wound. Secondly, Pearse clearly identified with specific Irish revolutionary models. Emmet was the most personally sympathetic. His youth and ardour, the 'nobility' of his stances and the pathos of his end, represented the very qualities and conditions which Pearse wished to emulate. Nevertheless there could be no question, in Pearse's mind, as to the supreme model. It was Tone who not only participated largely in Emmet's more appealing traits and type of fate, but also possessed originality of mind, intellectual acumen, earthy actuality and an indomitable gaiety of spirit. Over and above all this, he was the Founding Father.

In fact, Pearse was in no small way responsible for the elevation of Tone to the eminence which he has enjoyed in the revolutionist canon in the present century. Tone had of course long held a leading place in his canon. Apart from the firm shape which he had given to the insurrectionary creed in the 1790s, he had been well promoted by his own family; and, in his posthumously published *Life* (1826) and *Autobiography* (1826), he had served as his own best advocate. Somehow, he managed to transfer his charm and endearing energy and hope from life to print. But it was Pearse, much more than any other, who was responsible for Tone's virtual sanctification, and for rendering him at once the St Paul and the St Augustine of Irish revolution.

VI

Thus, the ideology of violence in Ireland may be said to have developed in five stages. Others, even if they agreed with such an episodic stylised view, might well select another range of steps for special emphasis; and no less than anybody else, I realise that this type of analysis leaves aside the incremental, gradual and interactive aspects of the development of doctrine and its associative rhetoric and image. Still, I have deliberately attempted to distinguish, and then atomise, the main or critical elements which have gone into the making of the modern Irish revolutionary mind because this seemed the most effective way of discovering, and pinning, the *mélange*.

From the agrarian societies of the eighteenth century came the general habituation to the use of force and conspiracy, and the concepts of alternative law and rule. From Tone derived the clear expression of the dogmas that the British connection was the unfailing source of Ireland's ills, and that 'Protestant, Catholic and Dissenter' was a false distinction, employed by the imperial power to divide Irishmen, for their better subjugation. Tone also contributed the notion of the Republic (especially as epitomised by its Army, the repository of civic virtue and authority), and in general fathered the movement's totalitarian strain. From the Young Irelanders came the first definite association of cultural separation, mass education and popular literature with the cause of violence. To them too we must attribute the first clear linkage of political virility and the use of arms. From Fenianism came the assertion that Ireland was in a constant state of war with Britain, as well as the assumption of governmental rights by the Irish military arm which was committed to that struggle. It was Fenianism moreover which developed the strategy of manipulating Irish opinion by evocative demonstrations and the tactic of infiltrating and deploying exterior organisations. From Pearse came the 'religion' of violent nationalism, the cults of blood, youth and sacrifice, and the concepts of generational witness, historic roles and the supremacy of the gesture.

Clearly, no single revolutionary Republican 'mind' ever reconciled all these disparate elements. Perhaps no single mind could even hold them all together at any time. But they do constitute a syndrome. The balance and emphasis may vary wildly from person to person. But no one dedicated to the politics of violence in Ireland will have been untouched, in some degree or other, by the items in this particular congery. Nor was, or is, their effect confined to those who affect violence. One of the lasting strengths of politics bellicose in Ireland is the emotional pull which it has ever exercised upon politics constitutional. Those who are confounded by the contradiction know little of human nature. Let them ponder slowly Boswell's reflection upon the '45:

The very Highland names, or the sound of a bagpipe will stir my blood, and fill me with a mixture of melancholy and respect for courage; with pity for an unfortunate and superstitious regard for antiquity and thoughtless inclination for war; in short, with a crowd of sensations with which sober rationality has nothing to do.[20]

Chapter 6

Politics Clerical

I

It is perhaps most revealing to pursue the ambiguities of constitutional politics, and their uneasy and shifting relationship to violence, at a humble level. The major movements and the great men show these boldly, but crudely. The delicacies and detail reveal themselves under the microscope. For beneath the grand obfuscations of the nineteenth-century crusades lay a mass of minute individual ambivalence. Possibly the best means of all of disentangling this intricacy may be to analyse its operation in the Catholic priesthood from 1830 onwards. Not that the priests were unique in their political ambiguity. On the contrary the great majority of their flocks shuttled, in precisely the same fashion as themselves, between sets of contradictory impulses. But partly because of their role as local leaders, and partly because the pressures making for contradiction were especially direct and powerful in their particular case, the priests exhibited these forms of ambiguity in a much heightened way.

The Catholic Church was first harnessed to Irish politics by O'Connell. He forced it into alignment with the popular agitation on the veto issue in the years 1809–15, and into a positive and active alliance in the Catholic Association from 1824 onwards. The Catholic Relief Act of 1829 and the dissolution of the Association, should, in logic, have terminated the alliance; and the episcopate in general intended that it should. But O'Connell's support of the Whigs, with a few short estrangements, throughout the 1830s had irresistible attractions for the Church. The main practical benefits promised by the tacit agreements with the Whigs – the abolition of the tithes paid to the Anglican Establishment in Ireland, full civil equality, a diminution of the Protestant Ascendancy, and the opening to Catholics of some of the doors to local place and power – were all sufficiently 'religious' in character to draw even the prelates back to the electoral struggle. Bishop Nolan of Kildare and Leighlin was typical of his brethren when he wrote, the eve of the general election of 1835, that although he wished his clergy to eschew all political activity whatever, this was not practicable immediately. The Tories were working to sustain Protestantism, continue the inequity of an Established Church and hold back necessary social and economic reforms. In these circumstances, the clergy had no choice but to muster every Catholic vote behind the Whigs: 'we are bound to give them [the laity] our assistance by instruction, advice, exhortation, and it is necessary to explain to the electors the real nature of the question which they are now called on to determine by their votes'.[1] This pious apologia should not blind us to the fact that a roaring political animal had been awoken in many priests and bishops. With his usual acuity, de Tocqueville discerned this when he dined with Nolan in Carlow in the same year:

> An archbishop was there, four bishops and several priests. . . . The conversation turned on the state of the country and politics. The feelings expressed were extremely democratic. Distrust and hatred of the great landlords; love of the people, and confidence in them. Bitter memories of past oppression. An air of exaltation at present or approaching victory. A profound hatred of the Protestants and above all of their clergy. Little impartiality apparent. Clearly as much the leaders of a Party as the representatives of the Church.[2]

The clerical re-engagement in O'Connell's repeal campaign in the early 1840s was more difficult to reconcile with spiritual needs than had been the participation of the preceding decade. Yet fully two-thirds of the Irish bishops and a still higher proportion of the lower clergy eventually threw themselves into this agitation. Even the non-combatant third of the episcopate did not overtly or specifically oppose repeal; and some of them held back on tactical grounds alone. Doubtless the explanation of this pugnacious response was in part commonplace, instinctive nationalism; in part, disenchantment with the meagre gains of the 1830s from the strategy of alliance with a British party; and in part, a sudden hope of Catholic predominance, or at least 'due influence', in a substantially autonomous nation.

The collapse of the repeal movement and O'Connell's death did not diminish clerical influence in Irish politics. The appetite had grown with feeding, and in many ways the Church was more powerful politically, even if less coherent in its aims, in the immediate post-famine years. The failure to maintain or rebuild a secure national party had left a vacuum which, to some degree, the priests and bishops filled. Besides they had grown more triumphalist in attitude with the successive decades of comparative success. 'By 1850, then', O Faolain writes, 'that terrible bogyman of the nineteenth century "the priest in politics" has arrived in Ireland.' He had been on the way for quarter of a century, at least.

None the less priestly power was to some extent contingent on the absence of lay. In this sphere, no less than the sphere of slogans and images, Parnell and Home Rule served as the evening performance of O'Connell and repeal. From 1881 on, the Church, almost *en bloc*, was embedded in and integral to the Parnellite movement – subordinate no doubt but also accorded the respect and accommodation earned by its indispensability as sanctioner of popular courses and local agent of the organisation. The aftermath, following Parnell's overthrow and death, once more repeated substantially the earlier experience. The badly co-ordinated but vigorous clerical 'interference' in the politics of the 1890s matched that of the 1850s very closely – except of course that it produced a more generally hostile reaction among the rejected faction of the Nationalists. Nearly thirty years on, the Church again proved itself indispensable politically. Not only was it a necessary element in the anti-conscription campaign of 1918, it even took the initiative, at any rate in the form of an attempted pre-emptive strike. On 9 April 1918, some hours before Lloyd George announced his proposal to extend compulsory military service to Ireland, the standing committee of the Irish hierarchy declared:

> Had the government in any reasonable time given Ireland the benefit of the principles, which are declared to be at stake in the war, by the concession of a full measure of self government, there would have been no occasion for contemplating forced levies from her now. What between mismanagement and mischief-making this country has already been deplorably upset, and it would be a fatal mistake, surpassing the worst blunders of the past four years, to furnish a telling plea now for desperate courses by an attempt to enforce conscription.[3]

Thus, although role, function and degrees of application and effectiveness varied greatly from phase to phase, the 'Church-in-politics' was a constant factor of first importance in Ireland throughout the last three-quarters of the nineteenth century, and even in the first two decades of the next.

The 'Church-in-politics' in the nineteenth century meant clerical influence rather than dictation, and clerical influence did not mean clerical intimidation; this was rare. Essentially, it had three other sources. First, many men looked to their priests for advice on how to vote. This should occasion no surprise. Not for nothing do historians speak of the age of deference. Guidance from superiors (the very word is redolent of the period) was not only accepted, but also widely sought. Although this was a factor of diminishing force after 1850, the events of the last decade of the century showed that it was far from dead even then. Secondly, and no less true for being a commonplace, the priests provided local leadership. This leadership had a formal aspect, as in the headship of committees and deputations. But much more significant was the priest's role as articulator of popular aspirations and purposes. Not infrequently, the very forms and formulae determined the character of political action. Finally, and most important, the clergy largely controlled, even in the Parnellite party of 1881–90, the selection of parliamentary candidates; and down to 1872 at least, they were largely responsible for canvassing the electors, for getting them to the polls and for ensuring that they voted as directed. In the age before modern party discipline in Parliament or party machinery in the constituencies – that is, broadly speaking, down to 1880 – these functions gave the priests considerable, though by no means overwhelming, political power. To some extent, the bishops shared in this direct influence through voter-guidance, the shaping of opinion and the choice and support of parliamentary candidates. But the essence of their political influence lay, not in these fields, but in their authority over their priests, and in their capacity for joint action. The one gave them, in favourable circumstances, a decisive influence over those who influenced the public in the parishes. The other might give them, in favourable circumstances, a decisive influence over national policy.

Yet the Church had peculiar difficulties in the exercise of this extensive power. In three particular ways, it was tied to the course of caution. First, the authoritarian structure favoured age, and increasingly so as the nineteenth century wore on, and the average age of parish priests – none of whom retired – rose steadily. The bishops at the apex of the system were generally old men; and although there were generational modifications from the extreme timidity of the early nineteenth century, and although there were always a few like MacHale of Tuam or Croke of Cashel who kept their early fire, the episcopate as a whole was almost always more conservative than the subordinate priests. Secondly, several of the first professors at Maynooth were French *émigrés*; and whatever of their much-vaunted importation of Jansenism, they undoubtedly stamped Gallicanism – in the sense of respect for royal institutions and lawfully constituted authority – upon the courses in dogmatic and moral theology, in which more than half the Irish parish clergy of the nineteenth century were trained. 'Dr D'Anglade and Dr De la Hogue . . . were the passive obedience men, the Sibthorpes and Mainwarings [the High Church Tories] of Maynooth'.[4] Thirdly, ultra-montanism, in the form of Pope and propaganda, pressed the Irish clergy extremely hard towards loyalty to the Crown and abstention from political activism, let alone political radicalism. From 1809 onwards, the British government could and did exert very great pressure upon the papacy to render the Irish Church submissive; and generally Rome, with larger fish to fry in other British pans, responded readily enough.

On the other hand, the Irish priests were almost without exception born, bred and schooled in the nationalism of their respective early days. Moreover, during the second and again in the last quarter of the nineteenth century, Catholicism and nationalism were virtually interchangeable terms – for the Catholic masses at least; and herein the priests' interest as an order marched with their predilictions as men. Last but far from least, by the apparent paradox which was no more than a truism, after all, their local leadership of their congregations depended on their heading in the same direction as the led. A priest deviating in public purpose from his people soon lost all influence in, and even most of his income, from his parish. Indeed, not so very long before, priests challenging the Rightboys had actually lost their congregations temporarily into the bargain.

Thus, clerical power called for great delicacy in practice. Each of its wielders, curate, parish clergyman, monk, friar and bishop, was subject to pressures from opposite directions. The clerical dilemma was particularly acute whenever Irish nationalism veered towards conspiratorial organisation or the advocacy of physical violence. But even the constitutional movements were by no means free from difficulty. Here the first lessons in evasion and illusive capework had to be learnt.

II

As we have seen, the Irish episcopate evidently determined against further political engagement after the Catholic Relief Act was passed in 1829. In a joint statement of 1830, drawn up by Bishop Doyle of Kildare and Leighlin, they counselled all clergy to keep aloof from political activity of every kind in future; and in the following year, the priests of the ecclesiastical province of Leinster were forbidden to allow any ecclesiastical building to be used for political purposes. This was of first importance, as churches were then the normal and often the only possible meeting places for Catholics in politics. Meanwhile, there was no episcopal – and, it would seem, no significant clerical – support for O'Connell's first repeal agitation of 1830–1. In fact, in the Leinster province, most bishops positively refused to countenance repeal and although Doyle was more equivocal (he appreciated the danger of alienating his priests and the laity), he privately opposed repeal in 1831, and worked against the repeal candidates in Ireland in 1832. Doyle was arguing already that repeal was the enemy of reform, and that the most promising tactic was the Whig alliance, with as many concessions as possible to the Irish demands to be exacted as the price.

In the same strain, in January 1834 the entire Irish hierarchy at a synod in Dublin passed two resolutions unanimously, one, repeating in stronger terms the injunction of 1830 that priests stay clear of politics and concern themselves solely with their spiritual vocations, and the other making generally applicable throughout Ireland the Leinster prohibition against the use of church buildings for any secular purpose 'except in cases connected with charity or religion'.[5] These resolutions were detailed and precise, though whereas the second, concerning church buildings, was an absolute and mandatory instruction, the first was merely a 'most earnest' recommendation to the clergy to observe what the bishops had agreed on. Had these instructions been adhered to, the repeal movement of 1840–3 could scarcely have got off the ground.

Almost immediately, however, the resolutions were broken wholesale in spirit or letter. The dividing line between the political and secular, on the one hand, and the religious and charitable, on the other, proved mercifully elastic. For example, when in October 1834 Bishop Blake of Dromore presided over an O'Connell tribute meeting held in the grounds of his cathedral, he argued that all was in accordance with the resolutions, first, because the meeting took place outside and not within the church, and secondly because rewarding O'Connell for his past exertions was a charitable and not a political affair! This neatly illustrates one sort of evasion. Another type was shown, as we have seen, in January 1835 when Bishop Nolan in the very 'act' of upholding clerical abstention from politics, ordered his clergy to fight the Tories in the general election because they were an anti-Catholic confederation. Thus, hardly had the synodal resolutions of 1834 been published than it was made quite clear that they constituted no obstacle to the renewal of national clerical organisation for almost any likely legislative object. 'Religion and charity' might be stretched to cover most political action in contemporary Ireland; and the sins which charity failed to cover might be safely left to the casuists to explain away.

From 1835 to 1839, however, no difficulties of moment arose in this sphere. O'Connell was then the leading advocate of and actor in the Whig alliance, which the clergy generally favoured. But in the spring of 1839, Rome intervened for the first time since 1815 to remove the Irish Church from politics. Hitherto Gregory XVI, Pope since 1831, had normally accommodated the British government in filling Irish bishoprics and other senior ecclesiastical positions. But there had been no direct intervention. Now Cardinal Fransoni, the Prefect of Propaganda, wrote two letters to the Irish primate, Crolly, concerning reports that MacHale and other Irish bishops were presiding over political banquets, denouncing the government and exciting popular passions. Crolly was instructed to dissuade them not only from political activity but from even all *semblance* of political involvement, and to remind them that 'they have been sent not to pursue eagerly that ways of the World and the activities of political parties, but to weep without remission between the porch and the altar in the misfortunes, so many and so great, of the persecuted Church'.[6] These letters were not made public at the time, but the contents were communicated to all the Irish bishops and possibly to other members of the Irish clergy. Fransoni's letters, of course, practically repeated one of the synodal resolutions of 1834, and to that extent introduced no novelty. But the fact that Rome had taken a hand once more in the Irish domestic conflict seemed likely, sooner or later, to produce a new embarrassment.

The Fransoni letters had no immediate effect. As soon as O'Connell began serious campaigning, in 1840, several bishops, headed by Mac-Hale, declared publicly for repeal, and actively engaged in the struggle as O'Connell's allies. In all their dioceses the mass of the clergy joined and worked for the Repeal Association; to a lesser extent the same was true even in 1840 in dioceses still 'neutral' or covertly hostile, so far as their various lordships were concerned. Over the next three years, other members of the hierarchy committed themselves to the cause. Eleven more became members of the Association, most of them zealous parti-

sans into the bargain. This accounted for the considerable majority of the
Irish bishops; and in their dioceses the priests were active repealers
almost to a man. The Fransoni injunctions were simply ignored, a
practicable course when their existence was known only to the higher
clergy.

But in 1844 the British government persuaded Rome to enter the scene
again, this time quite openly. Working directly through British agents in
Italy and indirectly through Metternich, Peel and Graham induced the
Pope to reprove publicly all those members of the Irish clergy who had
involved themselves in political agitation, that is to say, two-thirds of the
Irish bishops and a still higher proportion of the ordinary priests.
Although the papal rescript of October 1844 was milder than Peel had
hoped – it contained no threats of punishment – it was none the less
severe. The injunction of 1839, it complained, had been ignored, to the
discredit as well as the sorrow of the Holy See. Ecclesiastics were sternly
reminded of their sacred duty to separate themselves from all secular
concerns, and by word and example to inculcate subjection to the temporal power in civil matters, and to dissipate popular excitements. Crolly
was instructed to admonish all ecclesiastics, and especially all bishops,
who defied this teaching.

As if in jest, it was two of the most rabid episcopal repealers, who
proposed and seconded a resolution, passed unanimously at the national
synod of November 1844, that the rescript be received with 'profound
respect, obedience and veneration', and that 'they all pledge themselves
to carry the spirit thereof into effect'.[7] One says 'jest' because the rescript
passed rippleless across the Irish scene. No priest or bishop ever felt
called on to resign from the Association because Rome had spoken; few
even reduced the ardour of their banquet orations. How was this possible? The recalcitrants used two lines of self-justification. The first was
expressed by Cantwell of Meath as follows: 'Some Bishops (they were
only a few in number) understood the letter as implying a prohibition to
take any part in a public meeting, or to be present at a public dinner. . . .
We (the majority) inferred, and I think we were justified in the inference,
that conduct and language at all times unbecoming our sacred characters
and not presence on such legitimate occasions were the objects of the wise
and salutary precaution'. The duties of the priesthood 'are not incompatible with the clergy taking a moderate and prudent part in meetings
convened for the purpose of promoting the spiritual and temporal wel-
fare of their flocks'.[8] The other line of justification, that while the
rescript expressed sound doctrine, it was not applicable to Irish circumstances, was put forward by Higgins of Dromore. Dismissing the rescript of 1844 as 'very harmless', Higgins observed, 'We receive the
document with the profoundest respect . . . but being purely hypothetical, it leaves matters precisely as they stood before'.[9] Surely Cantwell and Higgins were disingenuous. The offensive speeches which the

rescript quoted, and on which it had been based, had included several of their own; and all 'secular' activity for whatever cause, had been unreservedly condemned. *O sancta simplicitas*: almost heavenly obtuseness was required to interpret the document as endorsing or even regarding with complacency the behaviour of the episcopal repealers.

Doubtless the repeal bishops had their justifications. Their motivation was mixed, but one of its elements, as Cantwell indicated, was a view of man as a totality, in which such 'civil' matters as poverty and human dignity were no less a priest's concern than prayer and preaching; and the fierce lay reaction to the Archbishop of Dublin's tentative use of the rescript to try to wean his clergy away from agitation shows how deep the alienation of priests and people, and perhaps also of priests and prelates, might have gone, if the entire hierarchy had behaved as propaganda directed.

On the other hand, the bishops of the 1840s were, under pressure, exhibiting two classic forms of clerical ambiguity in their dealings with the higher authority of Rome. First, while protesting that they obeyed the letter of the decree, they construed that letter in a wildly favourable, not to say wholly implausible, sense. Secondly, while ostensibly embracing the decree without reserve, they argued that it was totally inapplicable in Irish circumstances. These were not the only responses of threatened bishops in the mid-nineteenth century. We have already noted the types of evasion exemplified by Blake's scholastic distinctions and Nolan's Catholicising of issues of power. There was also more downright opposition. On the education question of 1845–50, it was said of Bishop Ryan of Limerick that when he was told 'the Pope commands a thing, he replies that the Pope does not know the state of his diocese';[10] and on the same matter, Walsh of Ossory simply deployed canon law against Rome itself by rejecting rescripts as forceless because they were not preceptive. But such open defiance was rare. In general, either the Cantwell or the Higgins line of evasion or avoidance was employed throughout the remainder of the nineteenth century, and never more markedly than during the 1880s when the Home Rule and Land League campaigns reproduced, often almost exactly, the ecclesiastical crises and escapes of forty years before.

III

The priests and bishops had, however, a second front to defend. The formal subordination to the Vatican was but one aspect of the Irish Church's difficulties. The counterpart, its relationship to its nationalist congregations, created still more embarrassment. This was so even in the most constitutionalist of phases. But when the secret society, the revolutionary ideal and the specifically *republican* objective (with all its Jacobinical connotations as well as its direct repudiation of authority) were in the ascendant, the problems multiplied. How then did the Church hold the uneasy balance when these elements were rising or dominant in Irish nationalism? By, I would suggest, a triple ambiguity.

The first face of this ambiguity may be termed the 'recessional'. As nationalistic violence receded in time so might it be the more safely sanctioned: 'the more ancient the patriots,' Dr J. P. P. O'Shea has written, 'the more hearty . . . retrospective benediction'.[11] Bloody resistance to Cromwell or the Williamites was plainly glorious. Nor was there very long to wait before even bloody resistance to George III was baptised. Within fifty years of its outbreak the Leinster rising of 1798, though execrated and repudiated by almost the entire Irish episcopate in its own day, was being held up as a noble contrast to the irresponsible vapourising of the Young Irelanders. When the Young Ireland rebellion of 1848 took place – almost literally in a cottage at Ballingarry – contempt for the 'cabbage-garden' rising was added to the general clerical detestation of the movement. Yet thirty years later Archbishop Croke, the bellwether of advanced clerical nationalism – theoretically even a revolutionist, though a revolutionist for whom it was always jam tomorrow or jam yesterday, but never jam today – unblushingly praised the patriotism of the people of Ballingarry to their faces. Similarly, when in the mid-1860s the Church was in full cry in denouncing Fenianism, the open 'nobility' – 'nobility' was the almost inevitable encomium of dead and buried revolution – of Young Ireland was made to stand in bold relief to the hidden, dark and squalid machinations of the new conspirators. In turn, in 1886, a Nenagh priest condemning the left-wing capture of the Gaelic Athletic Association, was to declare:

> I have mentioned [the Fenians] and I ask you to give me a cheer for their names. I admire those men, I know they were honest and true. Can I say the same of those who [today] . . . would lead the youth of Ireland into the way of ruin and restore again the golden age of informers? [12]

Meanwhile, the hagiography of the Irish revolutionary tradition was becoming a settled thing, enshrined in particular in the Sullivans' stirring compilation, *Speeches from the Dock* (1867). By none were the classic perorations of heroic violence – from Robert Emmet's 'When my country takes her place among the nations of the earth, *then* and *not till then*, let my epitaph be written' to the 'God save Ireland' of the Manchester Martyrs in 1867 – by none were these declaimed more ringingly from platforms and dining tables up and down the country than by priests and political prelates.

The second face of clerical ambivalence was the gestural, the gestures which carried no dangerous consequences within themselves. Let me employ as an illustration the visit of the Prince of Wales to Ireland in 1885, during a phase of political repression. A considerable portion of the

Church supported a boycott of His Royal Highness. Privately, Croke favoured receiving the prince, but he dared not fly in the face of excited popular opinion. In public he proposed, in subtle compromise, that his clergy should proffer only 'the charity of their silence'.[13] More typical however of the open reaction of the patriotic priests was the call of a Fr Condon, 'shame on the Irishman who would wish to see English Royalty defiling our shores, especially when it plants its unholy presence in the person of the . . . Prince of Wales'.[14] Of course, men like Croke had to think, in high tactical terms, of the Nationalist Party's relationship with Gladstone. But the rank-and-file clergy could on the not infrequent occasions of this kind, both give vent to their inherent anglophobia and participate in national posturing in complete security.

Humanitarianism was the third stamp of priestly ambivalence. Perhaps humanitarianism is not the exact word: what one really needs is a compound embracing sympathy with suffering, the distinction between a man and his beliefs, and elemental tribal identification. In the aftermath of Fenianism, the clergy, having anathematised it while it was a brooding force, began to bless it increasingly when extinguished. At least in the getting up of petitions for the amnesty of particular prisoners – the 'unwise but afflicted Fenians', as one priest delicately described them – and in chairing meetings of the Amnesty Association, large numbers of priests strove to box the Irish ideological compass. The execution of the Manchester Martyrs, who were after all avowed members of the IRB condemned to death for the shooting of a policeman, provided the most important opening for clerical ambivalence, in the flood of funeral processions, demonstrations and requiem services which it released in 1868. 'For the first time during years', wrote A. M. Sullivan, 'the distinction between Fenian and non-Fenian Nationalists seemed to disappear'.[15] In April 1869 the *Dublin Review* neatly captured the new Janus-faced stance of the clergy. Fenianism, it said,

> has been able to present itself before the world . . . as if it had . . . the sympathy of strong sections of the Catholic clergy. This sympathy has certainly only been a kind of posthumous sympathy, limited to such objects as the saying of Masses for the souls of executed Fenians, or the collections of funds for the relief of the families of incarcerated Fenians. Still, it marks a difference . . . which it would be idle to ignore.[16]

Still more striking perhaps was the revision in the clerical attitude towards two specific Fenians as time and, later, death blurred their offences. James Stephens was, as we have seen, the chief begetter of Fenianism, Charles Kickham its most fearless defender against ecclesiastical condemnation. Yet when in 1885 Stephens returned to Ireland, impoverished and rejected by the French republicans, some priests presided over the meetings of sympathy, and many contributed to the fund for Stephens's relief. As ever the well-poised Croke struck the perfect balance. In subscribing £5 to the relief fund, he eulogised Stephens's selfless patriotism, adding however that he had ever been 'a deluded lover of his country'.[17]

Similarly, by the later 1870s Kickham's anti-clericalism was slipping out of mind, and priests were lauding publicly his fortitude and self-sacrifice. Several even contributed to a testimonial raised for him in 1878. Among the contributors was Croke. This action, taken in conjunction with the rest of his veering course in 1878, so epitomises the humanitarian dashes against 'reason' by the priests that it is worth some particular examination. Earlier in that year, Croke had also contributed to a general fund for the support of amnestied Fenian prisoners. His cheque was accompanied by these words, published, as they were meant to be, in the newspapers:

> They suffered long and much for the patriotic faith that was in them, and the country for which they forfeited ten years of freedom is not likely to be unmindful of their patriotic captivity and privations.[18]

When remonstrated with by the Archbishop of Dublin, Cardinal Cullen, Croke defended himself boldly:

> I could never bring myself to rank Fenians as a body with Freemasons, for instance, for to make the great bulk of our Irish Catholic people, ninety per cent of whom are Fenian in heart or sympathy, answerable for the freaks and infidelity of a few amongst them.

He added that Cullen was wrong in supposing that the Fenians had achieved no good: 'They have given us a tolerable land Bill and disestablished the Protestant Church.'[19]

Yet only three months later Croke intervened strenuously in the Tipperary by-election *against* the Fenian interest and in support of the moderate Nationalist, E. D. Gray. Fenianism, in this context, seemed to him a deadly peril, and the contest a matter of life and death in Irish politics. 'I am essentially a non-politician', he began with disarming self-ignorance,

> but, sooner or later conclusions [will] have to be tried between Fenian, or advanced Nationalists [and the rest], and I believe the time has come when such a trial of strength may be opportunely made.[20]

The trial was made successfully in the event. As Croke reported delightedly to Cullen, 'Our election is over and our victory over the Fenians is complete'. His analysis of the triumph makes it clear that he saw Fenianism as the anti-Catholic interest.

Whenever there is or has been for years a foolish or lazy or unsympathetic priest, the Fenian element has been in the ascendant; whereas in every parish well worked, having Confraternities and everything else as it ought to be, the Fenian element is feeble and non-existent [sic].[21]

Thus, there can be no doubt that Croke, both as politician and churchman, was a relentless enemy of the IRB as a living organisation. But neither can there be doubt that in so far as its potency fell off, to precisely the same degree he allowed his instinct to identify with the characteristic emotions of IRBism full voice and play.

The greatest loss of potency was of course death itself. The best of all Fenians was of course the dead one. When Stephens himself died four years later in 1882 and the administrator of his native cathedral town refused to receive his body in his church, other priests ostentatiously marched with the funeral, and Croke in letters to the press expressed his deep regret that malignancy had pursued a patriot to the grave. Croke indeed helped both ecclesiastically and financially to provide a churchyard monument for Kickham soon after. Death has always been – if one may put it so – a towering element in Irish life; and the funeral and the memorial were natural and much-ploughed fields for clerical ambivalence. Masses for the souls, and high crosses to the memory, of the Manchester Martyrs were exactly the sort of outlets towards which the priests, otherwise held fast in bogs of authority, theology and expedience, rushed to express their inconstant passions.

IV

In all this the Church did not, as I have said, stand apart from the great body of its people. Its dilemmas were their dilemmas, albeit more acute in form. Its evasions were their evasions, albeit more public and more tortuous. One need look no farther than the very Parliamentary Party of the 1880s for a counterpart. Parnell's party was built upon impressions of violence, barely held back, in the wings; and on obeisance to revolutionism, provided that revolutionism was sufficiently distant in time or sufficiently personalised in its expression. When, in his 'radical' early speech in the United States in 1880, Parnell had spoken of paving the way for Ireland to 'take her place among the nations of the earth', no specific reference to Emmet or his armed rising was required. No Irish-American audience of the day would fail to catch and develop the revolutionary resonance of these words. Correspondingly, every meeting of the Parliamentary Party, every formal Nationalist gathering of any kind, in the last two decades of the nineteenth century ended with the singing of 'God save Ireland'. Of course, this was a most significant oblique assertion. Of course, the new anthem displaced – and was intended to displace – 'God save the Queen'. Of course, both repudiation of the Crown and the assertion of political parity and virility were implied. But so also was the essential link between the martyrs of violence in their generation, and the agitatory warriors of the present.

If then we feel ironic or scornful when we contemplate the systematic political ambivalence of the Irish Church, we should not halt at this particular limit but extend our contempt to Irish nationalism *en masse*. The priests were but the populace writ large. Not that the cold, disdainful eye should stay, even in this particular instance, at the Irish nationalists themselves. The matching and quite equal ambiguities of the British overlords and of the unionist semi-*colons* were an integral part of the difficulty. But, truly, irony and scorn would be misplaced. Pity, and tears for our fellow-shufflers, our fellow-victims of conflicting necessities, are more profitable, as well as more fitting, dispositions for historians. For we are dealing with an essentially colonial condition – or a doubly colonial one in the case of clergy with Roman flank also to defend. The colonial condition meant dependence, and dependency enjoined at once conformity and defiance. Conformity, in some degree to be experimentally established, was necessary for survival; defiance, in some degree to be experimentally established, was necessary for self-regard. Moreover, as the nineteenth century drew to its close, the national struggle became ever more ideational and sentimental in form. Increasingly, the conflict – and also the imperial resistance – moved into the arena of the subjective, of elemental feeling and antipathies. Thus we should look for the explanation of nationalistic ambiguity, at least in part, in terms of the sensibilities of subjection; and no sensibilities were more tender than those of the religious.

The Irish priests were peculiarly inhibited from sanctioning contemporary violence, conspiracy or separatist revolution. Dangerous or distasteful as these might seem to other Irishmen, they were still more firmly barred to this particular body by ecclesiastical discipline and training, and the overshadowing authority of Rome. In other words the Irish Catholic clergy were especially weak in the scales of relative power – that is, especially 'colonial' in condition. Yet this especial weakness probably explains the especial strength of such nationalistic declarations and stances as they could adopt. Again the explanation is fundamentally simple. In part, they were moved straightforwardly by their direct knowledge of their people's suffering. One fund to which Croke did not contribute in 1878 was for the relief of Turkish refugees; and he refused to do so, he wrote, not because the charity was unworthy but because

the Turkish fugitives . . . are not at all as much entitled to christian sympathy and support, as the poor, down-trodden, turnip-fed, and utterly miserable Irish peasants, who are being driven in desperation from their homes in the slushy slopes and wilds of the Galtee Mountains.[22]

This catches well the authentic note of compassionate anger which drove priests to separate themselves, on occasion after occasion, from the established governmental and social order.

But they were also impelled, in part, by the old fear of public divergence from their flocks; and in part, they were following the ordinary human path of striving to compensate for enforced restraint on one front by vehemence and exaggeration on another. But most of all the very fact that they *were* priests rendered them peculiarly sensitive to the perils of anglicisation, and to the importance of maintaining national distinctiveness. It was no coincidence that as Irish nationalism became less formally political and more cultural and tribal in basis in the 1890s, the clergy were to the forefront in every form of practical disengagement, from the Gaelic League to the Gaelic Athletic Association, and also in identifying Gaelicism generally with Catholicity. 'And why', asked a priest ironically in a clerical novel of the day, Canon P. A. Sheehan's *Luke Delmege*,

> did the Almighty create the Afghan and the Ashantee? [Was it] to be turned, in the course of time into a breeched and bloated Briton? . . . England's mission is to destroy and corrupt everything she touches –

It was this acute sense of Irish Catholic civilisation under threat, with British materialism and irreligion flooding in by the myriad roads of modern communications, which drove the clergy hardest towards identifying with the traditions of absolute resistance – always of course in the past or in the personal.

If this is true, and if the Church was here magnifying and clarifying instead of diverging from ordinary Irish nationalism, it follows that the orthodox Irish antitheses, constitutionalism and physical force, Home Rule and a republic, open and covert organisation, and the rest, are in some respect misleading. The ambiguities of a people in a colonial state are not constants, but reflect dualisms inherent or potential in almost every individual in that community. These ambiguities are so many ciphers for decoding attitudes and even action. They are no classifying device. On the contrary, they declassify, break up the boxes in which 'parties', 'factions', 'interests', 'sections' within a nationalism are ordinarily sorted. There is however the compensation that they take us to a deeper level of analysis. At this level there are few immutable commitments or objectives, and few final and absolute differences of feeling between the contending groups. And so we are often left, not with last season's pigeon-holes or glib polarities, but with the more difficult but also more truly fundamental problem of determining the reality in the ambiguous. As Yeats's final riddle in *Among School Children* puts it:

> O body swayed to music, O brightening glance,
> How can we know the dancer from the dance?

Chapter 7

The Politics of Gaelic

I

It seems clear that the Gaelic language was in rapid decline from, at latest, 1750. By 1801, when our statistical information effectively begins, only half of the population was monolingually Irish-speaking. Fifty years later this proportion had fallen to 5 per cent, and less than 25 per cent of Irish people could even speak the language. Fifty years later still, in 1901, the proportions were respectively 0.5 and 14 per cent. Moreover, the monolingual Irish speakers were now practically confined to the western and south-western seaboards. There were only *seven* monolingual Irish speakers left in the entire province of Leinster.

Fundamentally the explanation of the débâcle is simple. The major reason for the advance of English and the contraction of Gaelic – the two processes were practically if not necessarily linked – was the desire to survive in the modern world, or better still to improve one's lot. English was, practically, the sole language of administration, law, literacy and commerce. It was almost universally the language needed by the urban immigrant and the emigrant overseas. Conversely, Gaelic had become associated with ignorance, indigence, struggle and distress. Of course there were other agents at work in the transformation. As we shall see, the Catholic Church was more or less a negative collaborator. The national schools, from 1831 on, generally supported the parents in trying to rid their children of the language of poverty and replace it by one more materially advantageous. The politicisation of the masses (O'Connell's marvellous achievement of 1825–45) implied linguistic anglicisation upon a massive scale, for the language of agitation was almost invariably English. The million famine deaths must have been very largely the deaths of Irish speakers, for the great mortality was much the heaviest in the poorer and more remote regions. The rise of large-scale emigration, which to some extent *predated* the famine, cannot but have stimulated the passion to acquire English. The Protestant 'crusades' of the 1830s and 1840s to evangelise the Irish Catholic poor, which concentrated upon Gaelic-speaking regions, tended to identify, for a time, the Irish language with souperism and proselytising. But all these were either mere facilitators or comparatively trivial factors. The essential reason for the decline of Gaelic was the popular – or more precisely the Catholic popular – will.

II

Like many other features of Irish nationalism, the quest for Gaelic culture was largely Protestant in origin. It was by no means entirely so. Even in the mid-eighteenth century, there was a small body of Catholic cultural preservationists and revivalists, and they never lacked successors. But generally speaking the primary drives and work, down perhaps even to the formation of the Gaelic League in 1893, were Protestant. This is not to suggest of course that Gaelic sympathisers among Irish Protestants ever constituted more than a tiny minority. But all pre-League Gaelic movements were minute in scale; and in such lilliputian bodies, it was easy for Protestants to predominate, most of all in leadership.

Protestant Gaelicism had three main sources. The first was antiquarian, linguistic or local scholarship, or at least the patronage of such forms of inquiry, classification and collation. The educated gentleman of the later eighteenth century might well adopt such an interest: it was a European commonplace. Besides there were always some people of this class, as well as of other classes, who were simply curious about the past of their immediate regions, who simply wished to learn what they could about the ancient topography, the origins of the place names, the significances of the raths and cromlechs and the old familial and economic patterns of the places where they lived. The apotheosis, and the central and practical form, of this spirit was the Royal Irish Academy, founded in 1785. The Academy pursued, and directed the pursuit of, Gaelic studies as systematically and 'professionally' as any comparable continental institution of the day.

The second source was proselytism. Initially, the Anglican emphasis was placed on educating in English (manners, habits and identification as well as language) the rising generation of the Catholic poor. The Charter Schools, the first of which was set up in 1733, were the most ambitious – though also a very ineffectual – venture of this kind. By the closing decades of the eighteenth century, however, the use of Gaelic in evangelism had begun, not apparently, in the first instance, by the Church of Ireland proper, but by the Methodists. Men such as the Revd Charles Graham, 'the apostle of Kerry', and the Revd Gideon Ouseley, in the west, regarded the Irish language as their especial weapon, and execrated the priests who resisted their Irish bible and Irish preaching as indifferent to the Irish cultural heritage as well as idolators. Ouseley observed:

> The vitality of the Keltic languages among the small population of Wales, immediately joining the great population of England, as contrasted with the rapidity of its disappearance in the more numerous population of Ireland, separated by the sea from England, is one of the most striking illustrations of the effect of the Bible and preaching on the life of a language. In the Roman Catholic country, the want of the

Bible in the house, and the mother-tongue in worship, leaves a new language, if it has superior prestige, an open field for speedy victory.[1]

After 1800 an Anglican crusade for the conversion of the Irish peasantry rapidly gathered force, imitating to a large extent the technique of the Methodist pioneers of the 1790s. The effect was partly to align Protestantism and Gaelic in one camp, and Catholicism and the expansion of English in another. In 1838 Trinity College, Dublin, still substantially an Anglican seminary, established a Chair of Irish at the behest of the Society for the Promotion of the Education of the Native Irish through the medium of their own language. 'This Society', David Greene has observed,

> in spite of its innocent title was a missionary organisation and succeeded in provoking a reaction against the reading of the Irish bible, or, indeed any material in Irish at all, which was to do much harm in the already weakened status of the language.[2]

The third form of Protestant commitment to Gaelicisation – though it was far from being exclusively Protestant later on – sprang from the desire to find a native identification. Although there was no *necessary* connection between Protestantism and this third drive towards Gaelicisation there was certainly a natural affinity between the two throughout the nineteenth century, and especially in its last three-quarters.

Irish Protestants suffered a succession of blows between 1825 and 1845. The Catholic Relief Act of 1829 was followed by further 'surrenders' on tithes, police and local government, and by the opening of legal and public offices, on a considerable scale, to their former underlings. These last had been the work of the Whig governments of 1830–41. But still worse was to come. Peel's Tory administration of 1841–6 may have defied O'Connell successfully. But it gradually became clear that not only would there be no turning back of clocks under the Conservatives, but also that they would truckle shamelessly to the Catholic hierarchy in the hope of dividing the Irish national front. Thus, the ground on which the Anglo-Irish Ascendancy had stood for a century and a half was being cut away by both the growing power of their enemies at home and their 'abandonment' by their friends in Britain.

Those southern Irish Protestants, few perhaps in number but large in long-term influence, who acutely felt themselves to be second-class people within the British connection, or who foresaw that that connection would prove ephemeral, were well on the way to an identity crisis. One response was to escape to the indigenous civilisation. The Gaelic language, and the culture which it manifested and expressed, had the further, decisive advantage of pre-Christian (to say nothing of pre-Tridentine) origins. Irish Anglicans were alienated by an Irish nationalism which implicitly identified nationality with Catholicism. But a nationalism rooted not in a latter-day religion but in an immemorial past would break this particular connection. Of course such an impulse might express itself in various forms. Some Irish Anglicans argued that the Patrician Church had been a national rather than a Roman foundation: it was therefore they who had inherited the primitive Irish tradition, and the Catholics who were the recent innovators. For example, J. H. Todd in his celebrated *Patrick, Apostle of Ireland* (1864) aimed to advance 'our [the Anglican] real claims and our true position, as the Church of Patrick, Bridget and Columcille, and the only Church that possesses their true Comharbas [successors]'.[3] Other Irish Protestants looked back to the legendary world of the Irish sagas and found there the sources of a civilisation so ancient as to dwarf all modern differences in the timing of the waves of immigration, or in ecclesiastical or cultural forms. A verse of Ferguson's epitomised this striving to place natives and planters on the same level – their being equals at least in their common ignorance and neglect of Celtic antiquity –

> For, then, for them, alas, nor History best
> Nor even tradition; and the Now aspires
> To link his present with his Country's past,
> And live anew in Knowledge of his sires . . .
> A stranger in the land that gave him birth,
> The land a stranger to itself and him.

But others still – and these constituted the 'prophetic future' – chose the revival of the Gaelic language as the best mode of putting themselves on a par with the mass of their fellow-countrymen. Indeed they could view themselves as superior to that mass, who were busily discarding their cultural heritage and adopting the speech, life style and thought patterns of those to whom they remained politically opposed. Douglas Hyde gave the point its classical expression in 1892,

> the Irish race at present is in a most anomalous position, imitating England and yet apparently hating it. . . . It has lost all that they [the old patriots] had – language, tradition, music, genius and ideas. Just when we should be starting to build anew the Irish race and the Gaelic nation . . . we find ourselves despoiled of the bricks of nationality.[4]

Conversely, Catholic interest in the preservation or revival of Gaelic was comparatively slight until late in the nineteenth century. It was not that the Church was ever opposed to Gaelic as such. In 1768 the Bishop of Cloyne published an Irish dictionary in Paris expressly to help priests ministering in Irish-speaking areas. Seven years later the Irish episcopate informed the Pope that the students of the Irish College at Rome should be trained in both 'native' languages. Maynooth early possessed a Chair of Irish. But all this support was essentially utilitarian. Where the flock spoke only Gaelic, the priest must also do so if he were to be an effective pastor. It implied no effort to keep people Gaelic-speaking, or to prize the indigenous tongue. On the contrary, the bulk of the clergy probably shared the peasant attitude that Gaelic was the badge of poverty and failure. The case of John MacHale, Archbishop of Tuam from 1834 to 1881, is instructive. He was rare among the Catholic clergy of the early and mid-nineteenth century in his care for Gaelic. He translated into Irish from the classics and from contemporary English works and became first Patron of one of the earliest of the revival organisations, the Society for the Preservation of the Irish Language. He himself was the product of a hedge-school and a victim of a common 'type of barbarous co-operation between parents and teachers':

> although his father knew no English he was determined that the boy should speak English not only in school but at home. He hung around his neck a tally-stick which notched every time he spoke Irish, and he instructed the hedge school-master to punish him accordingly.[5]

Yet even MacHale urged his congregations to acquire the language of law, politics, business and advancement: 'Keep the Irish which is your own, and learn English.' Even at its most sympathetic, the mid-century Church in the stricken west was too close to the miseries of the people to try to insulate them, fatally, from the alien world.

III

Thus for almost the entire length of the nineteenth century the bulk of the pioneering work for the preservation of restoration of Gaelic culture is attributable to Irish Protestants. The first form of Protestant Gaelicism was dominated, before 1850, by George Petrie. Petrie, a member of the council of the Royal Irish Academy from 1829 on, played a leading part in the acquisition, collection and arrangement of early Irish manuscripts which provided the materials for the cultural 'renaissance'. He was also a path-finder in the scientific investigation of materials of another kind, early Christian architecture. Petrie was by no means alone in maintaining the tradition of Protestant Gaelic scholarship in the first half of the nineteenth century. Even if no other individual Protestant scholar of the day matched the foremost Catholics, Hardiman, O'Donovan and O'Curry, *collectively* Protestants could claim the lion's share of the early work of text gathering and similar primary tasks. Correspondingly, the tradition epitomised by Petrie, and centred in the Royal Irish Academy, was maintained by Church of Ireland divines, such as Todd and Charles Graves (successive presidents of the Academy in the decade, 1856–66) right through the nineteenth century. It is hardly too much to say, in fact, that Anglican clergymen dominated Old and Middle Irish scholarship until well into the twentieth. It is true that these men were essentially antiquarian in their interests, unconcerned with Gaelic as a living language. None the less, their labours both expressed some avowal of an

Irish identification and provided a sort of gold standard of serious erudition upon which the popularisers and propagandists could draw.

The second source of Protestant interest in Gaelicisation, the drive to proselytise among the Irish-speaking peasantry, did not long survive the great famine. Partly because of scandals and widespread relapses among the converted, and partly because of the dwindling of British financial support, the Irish Church Missions and other evangelical organisations declined rapidly in force in the 1860s. But the third source – the search for an Irish identity – was by then well in flow. In 1833 – the very year of Pusey's Assize sermon! – the young Samuel (later Sir Samuel) Ferguson, despairing of the British connection as a bulwark of their supremacy, concluded that the Anglo-Irish must save themselves by identifying thoroughly with the Irish past. 'Essentially, they should do this by taking the lead in recovering that past.' 'The Protestants of Ireland', Ferguson wrote,

> are wealthy and intelligent beyond most classes of their numbers, in the world; but their wealth has hitherto been insecure, because their intelligence has not embraced a thorough knowledge of the genius and disposition of their Catholic fellow-citizens. The genius of a people at large is not to be learned by the notes of Sunday tourists. The history of centuries must be gathered, published, studied and digested.[6]

Ferguson himself, however, lighted, not upon the 'history of centuries', but on the long-forgotten body of early Irish poetry and legend. Much of this, especially the Red Branch cycle centred on the heroic Cuchulainn, he translated into English prose or verse. It is not too much to hail him as the discoverer of the ancient Irish literature on which the later literary renaissance was to be based. Nor is it an exaggeration to speak of him as the inventor of a new sort of Anglo-Irish 'nationality'.

Ferguson's main successor was a son-of-the-rectory, Standish O'Grady, born in 1846. O'Grady stumbled on the same corpus of early literature as Ferguson had done, and on much the same line of reasoning as Ferguson's, but quite independently. To both, however, he brought a new vehemence of feeling and expression. His *History of Ireland: the heroic period* (1878–80), though derived from translated material, was the immediate source of the Irish literary revival of the 1890s, while his address 'to the landlords of Ireland' called upon them in apocalyptic terms to repent of their anglocentricity and to adopt and adapt the indigenous culture even at the eleventh hour. More important still was O'Grady's influence upon another son-of-the-rectory, Douglas Hyde. Hyde was no more O'Grady's direct pupil than O'Grady had been Ferguson's. But he came to manhood as O'Grady's work flowered and coloured the thought of some of the ablest of young Irish Protestants.

Meanwhile the Protestant identity crisis had also set off a movement of another and, politically, much more important kind. Here the critical single event seems to have been Thomas Davis's visit to Germany in 1839–40. This led him to redefine the concepts of 'nationality' and 'liberation'. They were no longer seen as a mere change in the management of the political and economic systems. The new emphasis was on *cultural* hostility. In the Irish case, the Gaelic language and 'way of life', 'racy of the soil', was central to the campaign.

Davis had drawn upon the works of Lessing, Fichte and the Schlegels and upon the example of Prussia whose genius, he wrote, having 'tossed in a hot trance, sprung up fresh and triumphant',[7] as soon as she had halted the advance of the French – culturally as well as militarily. He could not follow the model of nationality provided by the German Romantics completely. Where it stressed religion or ethnicity as bases of national identity, he had to part company. All else apart, such an emphasis could have left him, an Anglican and half-English in birth, stranded. Instead Davis presented Irish nationality as an organic growth, multi-confessional and multi-racial in character.

> At last we are beginning to see what we are, and what is our destiny. Our duty arises where our knowledge begins. The elements of Irish nationality are not only combining – in fact, they are growing confluent in our minds. Such nationality as merits a good man's help and wakens a true man's ambition – such nationality as could stand against internal faction and foreign intrigue – such nationality as would make the Irish hearth happy and the Irish name illustrious, is becoming understood. It must contain and represent the races of Ireland. It must not be Celtic, it must not be Saxon – it must be Irish. The Brehon law and the maxims of Westminster, the cloudy and lightning genius of the Gael, the placid strength of the Sasanach, the marshalling insight of the Norman – a literature which shall exhibit in combination the passions and idioms of all, and which shall equally express our mind in its romantic, its religious, its forensic, and its practical tendencies – finally, a native government, which shall know and rule by the arrogance of none – these are components of *such* a nationality.[8]

Such a view of nationality may not have been easily reconcilable with Gaelicisation, yet Davis proceeded to marry the two. 'To lose your native tongue', he wrote,

> and learn that of an alien, is the worst badge of conquest – it is a chain on the soul. To have lost entirely the national language is death; the fetter has worn through. . . . Nothing can make us believe that it is natural or honourable for the Irish to speak the speech of the alien, the invader, the Sassenagh tyrant.[9]

All this was paradoxical, to say the least. Davis himself was practically ignorant of Gaelic. His own father, a Royal Artillery surgeon stationed in

Ireland, could scarcely have been classified as other than in the service of the Sassenagh tyrant. Why the tongue of the Gael alone, at the expense of that of the Saxon or the Norman, should dominate in the commingled Irish culture was far from clear. Moreover, Davis was no Gaelic revivalist. On the contrary, he made it clear that the re-Gaelicisation of the English-speaking eastern parts of Ireland should not even be attempted in the nineteenth century, lest 'the reaction might extinguish it [the Irish language] altogether'. At most, he was a Gaelic preservationist, asking only for Irish-speaking teachers and Irish-translated books in the national schools of the still Irish-speaking districts (scarcely one-third of the entire country in 1843). His modest hope was to 'guard the language where it now exists, and prevent it being swept away by the English tongue, as the Red Americans have been by the English race from New York to New Orleans'.[10]

But despite all his limitation of objectives and confusions of thought, Davis, whether intentionally or not, riveted nationalism to cultural separation, and cultural separation to the Gaelic 'heritage' in general, and to the Gaelic language in particular. We might add that he riveted cultural separation and cultural hostility, for just as the German Romantics were hag-ridden by the fear of French cultural domination, Davis was hag-ridden by the fear of anglicisation. Where O'Connell opposed the retention of the Irish language as a barrier to economic development, constitutional advance and modernisation, Davis was anxious to retain it precisely because it was a barrier – to English influence. It was a short step from denouncing this influence because it was 'alien' to denouncing it *per se*, for its supposed characteristics of utilitarianism, industrialism, urbanisation and the like. Sooner or later, Gaelic would be seen as an offensive as well as a defensive weapon in the armoury of Irish nationalism; and sooner or later some would see that nationalism as essentially dependent on the Irish language.

Thus two strains of Protestant Gaelicisation, derived from alienation from Great Britain, developed in the second quarter of the nineteenth century. The Fergusonian (to be restated more forcibly in the next generation by O'Grady) sought merely to break any 'necessary' connection between Catholicism and Irish nationality and, conversely, any 'necessary' connection between Irish Protestantism and subservience to or identification with British interests. The shared ancient history and traditional culture of Ireland was to form the common ground on which the contemporary Irish factions might, to a degree, coalesce. This first strain was not explicitly political, let alone chauvinistic or revolutionary. But the second, or Davisian, strain was undoubtedly all three; and the later work of Douglas Hyde was to show, in its unintended consequences if not in its stated aims, that in any attempted mating of the two strains, the second was bound eventually to predominate.

In the last quarter of the nineteenth century, Hyde both dominated and redirected the Gaelic movement. Drawing, in effect, upon both the Fergusonian and Davisian strains of Protestant Gaelicisation, he attempted to render the resultant amalgam both practical and activist. He followed Ferguson and O'Grady in presenting the native language and culture as supra-factional and supra-sectarian, a field where Irish Protestant and Catholic could meet as equals in Hibernicism. To this end, Hyde insisted that political and religious subjects be altogether excluded from the language movement. On the other hand, he fully adopted and boldly extended Davis's concepts of cultural separation and hostility. He saw Ireland as in a state of war, in which her distinctiveness was steadily diminishing under the onslaught of British influences and example. The retreat was universal. 'The moment', Hyde wrote,

> Ireland broke with her Gaelic past she fell away hopelessly from all intellectual and artistic effort. She lost her musical instruments, she lost her music, she lost her games, she lost her language and popular literature, and with her language she lost her intellectuality.[11]

Hyde differed from Davis in three respects. First, his de-anglicisation campaign was proclaimed to be apolitical. Secondly, it was to take the offensive, to aim at the restoration of the vernacular language and the traditional life patterns over the entire country, where Davis's objective had been merely a holding operation. Thirdly, it was a programme of action rather than a *Nation*-like system of general exhortation. By propaganda, permeation, the building up of pressure groups and the manipulation of politicians and public bodies, a specific series of legislative and similar goals was to be attained. Correspondingly, Hyde eagerly supported the novel efforts of the revivalist organisations of the later 1870s and 1880s to standardise Irish as a contemporary language to speak in, and to hammer out a modern Irish prose style. As he himself put it, the aim was to render the present a rational continuation of the past. In short, Hyde was concerned to develop and promote a modern product for a modern market.

For all his realism in particulars, Hyde was unrealistic in general. It was impossible to confine the Gaelic League, of which he was the chief begetter in 1893, to the nurturing and expansion of the Irish language. In practice one could not long preach de-anglicisation without slipping into anglophobia, or proclaim a cultural crusade without slipping into a political and constitutional one. Hyde failed to avoid politics, even in the most ordinary of senses, partly because his movement was deliberately infiltrated and exploited by extremists, and partly because such a movement implicitly encouraged the idea of total separation. The League inevitably manufactured separatists. It also became a sort of school for rebellion, as well as an apparatus which knit sections of the middle and lower classes in the towns into a quasi-political association. Instead of binding Irishmen of all types and opinions together (as Hyde had originally hoped), it eventually drove the wedge between north and south, and unionist and Nationalist, deeper than ever, and gave new point and precision to Irish self-identity, externalising and symbolising what had hitherto been an inchoate aspiration in many cases.

It is difficult to believe that Hyde did not foresee, at all, these very likely developments. But his failure to do so would not have been incompatible with the traditions of Protestant Gaelicisation which he had inherited, run together, expanded and put to work. For these traditions were essentially inward-looking, concerned with the southern Irish Protestant's dilemma as Catholic nationalism waxed, and the British commitment to his interests in Ireland waned. There was of course much variety in the states of mind which these threats produced in those Protestants who chose to search for an Irish, as against a British, identification as a counter-measure. It would be misleading so to categorise the Royal Academical or evangelical devotees of Gaelic antiquity or the Gaelic language. Primarily they were the servants of either dead learning or spiritual rebirth. But even in these cases a deep respect for the native cultural achievement, and a sense of moral superiority to the natives who were busily jettisoning their inheritance, were clearly discernible. Occasionally, as with the Revd Maxwell Close, who, almost single-handed, maintained the Society for the Preservation of the Irish Language financially, or the Revd Euseby Cleaver, who, almost single-handed, paid for such Irish teaching as took place in Gaeltacht schools in the 1870s, a simple love of Irish for its own sake appears to have been the driving force. But the leading men, Ferguson, Davis, O'Grady and Hyde, all specifically recognised their dilemma and sought to escape it, in part at least, through the medium of Gaelic. As we have seen, their responses differed greatly in tack, emphasis and spirit. But they had this at least in common: each was an answer to a Protestant question. Not surprisingly, once these answers were sent abroad into a much larger world they took on new meanings. Ferguson and O'Grady, who remained unionists of a sort, had provided willy-nilly raw materials for cultural nationalism. Hyde, politically agnostic, had unintentionally furnished both dogma and an organisational network for radical republicanism. As for Davis, the preacher of Irish brotherhood and the power of educational enlightenment had innocently pointed the way to new Irish sources of fraternal hatred and pedagogical coercion.

IV

Although another Irish Protestant, Ernest Blythe, was to dominate the Gaelicising movement of the 1920s by virtue of his political office, the Protestant kingship of Gaelicisation effectively ended with Hyde. Indeed, even he was reduced to a pandering type of constitutional monarch once the Gaelic League had been launched in 1893. For in this field, as in others, Irish Catholics had become, by the late nineteenth century, sufficiently self-assured and practised to dispense with the traditional Anglo-Irish leadership, hitherto so common even in 'native' causes. This had been foreshadowed, as early as 1876, in the new Society for the Preservation of the Irish Language. Although essentially Protestant in inspiration, it elected a Catholic archbishop, MacHale, as Patron, and included a Catholic priest, Nolan, among its leading members. Clerical participation was still more evident and significant in the League. Eugene O'Growney, Professor of Irish at Maynooth, was not only one of Hyde's main coadjutors in the League's foundation, but also the composer of the textbooks for its educational programmes. Similarly, the Revd Patrick Dineen was the movement's lexicographer, the Revd Richard O'Daly a pioneer in the simplification of Gaelic spelling and its adaptation, for printing, to the Roman type, the Revd Peader Ua Laoghaire the prime mover in the use of colloquial Irish for literary work, and Fr O'Hickey (O'Growney's successor at Maynooth) the first successful champion of 'compulsory Irish' in education. It should be noted that all this priestly work, though often resting on sound scholarship, was essentially popularising and propagandist in character.

One may almost designate this a volte-face by the Church, for behind the leading priests–workers in the League stood many others, especially among the recent graduates of Maynooth and in the *corps d'armée* of the revival – the congregations of teaching brothers. How is the change to be explained? Clearly, one critical factor was the new sense, discussed above, that Irish Catholic culture and traditional rural life were under grave and rapidly mounting threat from anglicisation. Croke had sounded the toxin as early as 1884: 'England's accents', he declaimed, 'her vicious literature, her music, her dances, and her manifold mannerisms . . . [are] not racy of the soil, but rather alien, on the contrary to it, as are, for the most part, the men and women who first imported and still continued to patronise them.' [12] Over the next three decades, the polarisation of 'alien' and 'native' intensified, as did the double identification of 'native' with Catholic and Irish-speaking. In 1906 the Anglican Canon Hannay ('George Birmingham'), a member of the Gaelic League, was illegally excluded from participating in the organisation of a League feis by the parish priest of Tuam, Canon Macken, on the ground that he was fundamentally unIrish. Hyde interposed to save Macken: 'in view of the very ticklish situation in the archdiocese, and the certainty that to censure Macken would turn all the priests against it and kill the language, I think the CG [executive council of the League] will just let things be.' As George Moore later observed, 'Hyde has become the arch-type of the Catholic Protestant, cunning, subtle, cajoling, superficial and affable.' [13] To such a degree had Protestant Gaelgeoirs been driven on to the defensive, and to such a degree of influence had a

Catholic and even a clerical party risen in the language movement, by the early years of the present century.

The clearest identification of Gaelicism with Catholicism came, however, not from any priest but from a lay journalist, D. P. Moran, who had worked on the Gaelic League weekly in the late 1890s and founded his own highly influential weekly *The Leader* in 1900. Moran faced the question of the relationship of race, language and religion squarely. All three, he argued, were concentrated in the 'Gael'; and 'the Gael must be the element that absorbs. On no other basis can an Irish nation be reared that would not topple over by force of the very ridicule that it would beget.' [14] Thus, the Anglo-Irish were told bluntly that they must accommodate themselves, if not actually conform, to the native culture and religion. Only thereby could they qualify as members of the nation. 'Moran has been criticised for his alleged "racism" ', writes Dr D. G. Boyce,

But his real purpose was to spell out, regardless of cant and humbug, the principles which others accepted but preferred not to examine too closely. Moran denied that he was running a Catholic journal, or that he was maintaining that no one but a Catholic could be an Irishman. But, he retorted, 'when we look out on Ireland we see that those who believe or may be immediately induced to believe, in Ireland a nation are, as a matter of fact, Catholics'. 'In the main non-Catholic Ireland looks upon itself as British and as Anglo-Irish', he alleged; and those non-Catholics who would like to throw in their lot with the Irish nation's 'must recognise that the Irish nation is *de facto* a Catholic nation'. Moran had the unpleasant knack of stating clearly and unequivocally the direction in which the Gaelic movement was heading, and its implications for the 'English who happened to be born in Ireland'; any racial undertones were ones that he recognised, not ones that he invented.[15]

The attitudes which Moran expressed so truculently had to await the publication of Daniel Corkery's *Synge and the Anglo-Irish Tradition* for a systematic and 'academically respectable' formulation. But they were quite pervasive even in 1900–14; and if some Catholics were repelled when Moran presented them with his stark choices, more, doubtless, emerged from their reading of *The Leader* with 'raised consciousness' and a sense that their instinctive intuition of the Irish reality had been at last articulated and validated. The identity-crisis was no longer the plight, primarily, of the southern Irish Protestant. It was spreading fast. 'The question "who am I?" ', it has been well said, 'only arises when society does not comfortably answer it before it can be asked.' [16] Down to the collapse of Parnellism, with its appearance (or successful illusion) of a national front and of agreed primary national goals, Irish Catholic society had, by and large, answered this question comfortably before it could be asked. Thereafter, however, the revulsion from conventional parliamentary agitation and mere constitutional aims, coupled with intense cultural propagandising (striking with redoubled force for being so long restrained), strewed the identity crisis about in Catholic ranks.

For many *fin-de-siècle* Catholics, Gaelicisation provided an escape route from their newly perceived dilemma, as it had provided an escape route for some Anglo-Irish intellectuals over the past two generations. But for the more perfervid Catholics, Catholicism-in-nationalism was not one horn of a dilemma, but in itself a means of personal reintegration. For them, the Irish language, the Catholic religion and the ideology of political separation intermeshed. Thus, to the fear of 'modernisation' in its English form, and to the spiritual expansionism and missionary ardour which increasingly characterised the official Church, was added – for the laity at large – a sense that Gaelic was conterminous with Catholic, and Catholic with Gaelic, in Irish circumstances. By 1914 at least, the role-reversal was complete. Taking them as a whole, the Protestant communities of both south and north now felt not only alienated from, but even threatened by the Gaelic movement, as much perhaps for its Catholicisation as for its extreme politicisation.

V

The first steps in inserting Gaelic into the Irish educational system had been taken by the League's forerunner, the Society for the Preservation of the Irish Language. It wrung two concessions from Disraeli's second Conservative ministry: first, in 1878 the acceptance of 'Celtic' as a recognised subject for examination by the Intermediate Schools, and secondly, in the following year, permission to teach Irish in primary schools, albeit outside school hours. Doubtless these seemed, to a Tory administration, harmless concessions to quaint localism, committing nobody to anything. Twenty years later, however, the League succeeded in strengthening both provisions considerably, again under a Conservative government. Thanks to Hyde's influence over the 1899 Royal Commission on secondary education, the status of Irish in senior schools was raised markedly; and in 1900 Irish was allowed as a full primary school subject within school hours. Four years later, it was established as the main medium of primary teaching in the Irish-speaking districts. A critical advance was made when Irish was specified as a required subject for matriculation in the new National University of Ireland. This not only raised the language in reputation, but also introduced the novel element of compulsion. University entry, for most Irish Catholics, now depended – at least in theory – upon a certain proficiency in Gaelic. The League was launched on its coercive course. Simultaneously, it was being politicised, so rapidly in fact that by 1915 Hyde himself felt obliged to resign the presidency of a body which had become virtually a corps of the radical republican movement.

It was also true however that the radical republicans had become, to a considerable degree, Gaelicised. One of the ministries of the first Dail Eireann (1919) was a Department of the National Language, and its first minister none other than a former president of the Gaelic League, J. J. O'Kelly ('Sceilg'). In the midst of the Anglo-Irish war the League pressed an ambitious programme of Gaelicisation upon the underground government of the hypothetical independent state. In 1920 it proposed that all Irish schools (even those of Protestant Ulster, presumably) should teach alternately in Irish and English within two years, and be fully bilingual within five. The prospect of such a heroic attempted transformation terrified its destined instruments, the teachers. Comparatively few of them knew Irish, and not many of the remainder relished the struggle to acquire another language almost instantly. The upshot was a series of meetings between *inter alia* the teachers' union, the League and the Department of the National Language in 1921. The League programme was modified, but by no means emasculated. It was agreed that instruction in the 'infant' classes should be wholly in Irish, that at least one hour a day should be devoted to Irish in all other classes, and that from the age of 8 onwards teaching in certain subjects (a cynic might relish the selection: music, gymnastics, Irish history and Irish geography) would be wholly through the 'medium' of Gaelic. All this was worked out while the war was in its final phase; and the new state was barely in existence before, in April 1922, the government adopted and began to implement the revised programme. Meanwhile as early as August 1921 the Dail had agreed that the Gaeltachts, as the reservoirs of pure native culture, were to be preserved and supported at all costs. Only from these few scattered sources could national regeneration spread across the land.

What states of mind explain these extraordinary developments of 1919–22? After the Anglo-Irish war had ended in mid-1921, Michael Collins declared,

> We only succeeded after we had begun to get back our Irish ways; after we had made a serious effort to spread our own language; after we had striven again to govern ourselves. We can only keep out the enemy and all other enemies by completing that task. . . . The biggest task will be the restoration of the language.[17]

There could be no clearer evidence that a new orthodoxy, identifying political independence and national self-regard with the restoration of the Irish language, had been established. The Cumann na nGael governments of 1922–32 were full subscribers to this orthodoxy. For one thing, commitment to the language revival counteracted the pretensions of de Valera and the Republicans to being the sole custodians of true nationalism. For a second, two key ministers of these years, Ernest Blythe (of

Finance) and Eoin MacNeill (of Education, until the end of 1925) were zealots in the cause; and they could rely consistently upon the support of the powerful Minister of Defence, Richard Mulcahy. Mulcahy, in fact, was chairman of the Gaeltacht Commission of 1925, which assumed it to be 'the national duty', enshrined in the constitution of the Irish Free State, 'to uphold and foster the Irish language, the central and most distinctive feature of the tradition which is Irish nationality'.[18]

Blythe, the last of the great Protestant Gaelicisers (though an Ulster Presbyterian rather than a southern Anglican deviant from his group), was the key figure in the new revival. This was partly by virtue of the force of his convictions and the depth of his obduracy in the cause, and partly because of his influence over public expenditure in the parsimonious 1920s. Broadly, the strategy of the Gaelgeoirs in the government was threefold. First, the compulsory teaching of Irish in the schools was to produce in time – a very short time – a base of Irish speakers which would expand steadily as one age-group after another emerged from the system. This would be supplemented by state-subsidised Gaelic publishing, a state-subsidised Gaelic theatre, a large Gaelic component in the new radio service, 2RN, and similar intellectual and artistic supports, culminating in an 'Irish Academy'. The National University was to be pressed to move in the same direction, with the ultimate objective of instruction in Irish at the tertiary as well as the lower levels of education. Secondly, the Gaeltacht areas were not merely to be kept alive and intact by economic and technical aid and bounties, but also to be used as recruiting grounds for Irish speakers to man the educational and law enforcement systems, the civil and armed services, and local government. To this end, a network of Gaeltacht secondary schools and colleges was planned. Correspondingly, the engineers, doctors, judges, lawyers, priests and others 'servicing' the Gaeltachts should themselves be Irish speakers. Finally, the public sector was to be used, so far as practicable, to accomplish the transformation. Preference should be given, for example, to native speakers for entry to the civil service. Irish should be used in official business wherever possible, and various public appointments were to depend upon competence in the 'language'. In numerous other ways, the state's treasury of patronage and favours (vast by Irish standards) was to be put at the service of Gaelicisation.

Perhaps only Blythe, Mulcahy and MacNeill would have approved so draconian a programme. Yet the government as a whole accepted it in substance. Most of what was proposed was attempted, albeit with varying degrees of earnestness. What factors explain this extraordinary compliance? First, even if there were many more Dantons than Robespierres in the Treatyite party, most were willing enough to accept the end, a Gaelic Ireland, provided that it could be achieved painlessly – and by others. A generation of Gaelic League and similar crusading had left the majority of people in the Irish Free State (less than one-tenth of whom could speak Irish at this time) with the general feeling that nationality was in some sense or other dependent upon a native language and (more nebulously) a native culture. They would acquiesce, up to a point – to the point, at any rate, where it called for direct and palpable sacrifices from themselves – in the efforts of the enthusiasts to transform the speech and practices of their country. The politicians simply reflected the torpid preferences and inclinations of their constituents.

Secondly, the unchallenged decisions of the first Dail had become sacrosanct, all the more so after the sundering of Sinn Fein on the issues of treaty and Crown. The commitment to swift and thorough Gaelic-isation had been clearly made in 1919–22; and of all people the Treatyite politicians could least afford to be represented as covert West Britons after all. Strangely and suddenly, the 'revival' became a touchstone of serious patriotism. It was certainly a more desirable touchstone, to the Treatyites, than the 'republic'. Thirdly, the revival movement had touched a chord of folk memory in most Irish people. We are familiar enough with this proceeding in our own time, in the form of a search for 'roots' by resurgent communities. In Ireland the peeling off of even the outermost or most recent layers of anglicisation revealed a little of the pristine cultural landscape. Particular words and concepts became identifiable with their Gaelic originals; the Gaelic source of current speech patterns and constructions was discovered; old practices and styles of living, often mediated through the memories of parents and grandparents, were recalled and vivified; the land was repeopled, in imagination, by a pre-colonial society, free of the stains and shames of anglicisation. In short, Gaelicisation had a real, if shallow-rooted, emotional appeal: a compound of sentiment, nostalgia and idealisation constituted a genuine popular response. These three factors would seem largely to explain why such a government as Cosgrave's and such a chamber as the Dail of 1922–32 endorsed the main body of Blythe's wildly ambitious schemes.

It should be noted that the primary responsibility for Gaelicisation was placed upon three special groups in the community, the first two being teachers and children. The teachers could, to a limited extent, defend themselves against inordinate demands upon them. At the National Programme Conferences of 1921 and 1925–6 they managed to whittle down the more extravagant plans of the Gaelic League, and to secure more time for making the readjustments demanded of the profession. None the less, they won comparatively few concessions; indeed, all secondary school teachers had soon to pass an oral examination in the language before they would be 'recognised' by the Department of Education. Part of the explanation of the limited resistance is that the teachers themselves contained a higher proportion of Gaelic enthusiasts than any other body in the community (and this was steadily reinforced as the profitable accomplishment of 'proficiency' in Irish spread wider and

wider in the profession); and part, that various carrots, such as extra
financial grants for schools, higher salary payments for teachers or bonus
marks in examinations, were dangled before their noses. But the fact that
opposition to the decided state policy of compulsory Gaelicisation of the
schools was publicly stigmatised as unpatriotic was undoubtedly the
most important factor in the general acquiescence.

The children had no effective defence against the onward march of
compulsion, first, in the infant classes, where the entire instruction was
through Irish; next, in the later primary years, when the use of Irish as
the medium of instruction was advanced, step by step; and finally, in the
secondary schools, where Irish became an essential of the curriculum in
1928 and a necessary subject to pass in any Certificate examination by
1934. Compulsion certainly aroused antagonism. But just how much it is
impossible to say, in part because little was openly expressed or coher-
ently articulated even within families, and in part because it was counter-
balanced by the continuation of a vague, sluggish desire for Gaelicisation
among the great adult mass of non-participants. The system bore
heaviest of all upon those least capable of formulating or forming any
opposition, the 'infants' of 5, 6 or 7 years of age. The Ireland of the 1920s
and 1930s was largely innocent of child psychology. There was apparently no concern that little boys and girls should first encounter education in an incomprehensible tongue, which they heard only when the
school doors closed upon them in the morning. They had been selected as
the carriers of the national destiny: that was all.

There were, as the Revd S. O Cathain has observed, two fundamental
difficulties about basing a language restoration programme in Ireland
essentially upon the schools. First, the principal objective of the restoration movement was to produce fluent Irish speakers; it was a vernacular
that was to be revived, not just 'dead' reading and writing. 'But here the
teachers, in the secondary and to a lesser extent the primary schools,
came up against the crippling effects of the external examinations.' [19]
The educational system was organised about Certificates, even the
primary schools moving in this direction in 1929. This meant that Irish
was taught, essentially, for the set written test and not for verbal fluency,
with a correspondingly negative 'image' to add to that which it already
earned as 'compulsory'.

Secondly, very few people outside the schools could or would speak
Gaelic. There was practically no reinforcement in the community at large
(from which the children had emerged, in which they spent more than
half their time and to which they would eventually return) for what they
acquired painfully in the classroom. Even the Department of Education
reported in 1929, after nearly a decade of endeavour for the 'revival',

> as far as the general use of Irish is concerned, little progress seems to
> have been made in the last ten years. It appears to be true that very few

pupils speak Irish outside school hours, and a still smaller number can be still classified as Irish speakers a few years after leaving school. The Irish they have learnt is lost in the amount of English with which they have to deal on leaving school. English is the language of their sports and pastimes and of the means of earning their livelihood, while Irish remains a school subject closely allied to lessons and examinations. Under such circumstances it is inevitable that a very considerable part of the work done by the schools must fail to bear fruit.[20]

To this we might add the conclusion of the Irish National Teachers Organisation's (INTO) committee of inquiry into the use of Irish as a teaching medium (1936–41) that 'the results of the policy were in no way commensurate with the labour imposed on the teacher and the strain to which the children were alleged to be subjected'.[21] The Organisation's condemnations fell flat; practically, they were ignored. The system, as developed hastily and *ad hoc* in the 1920s, simply sat atop Irish education for the next forty years. It became in effect a sort of Irish weather, felt, vaguely, to be oppressive but inevitable. The forces which had enabled the 'revival' programme to take shape in 1921–2 remained operative, although in weaker form. Irish was still regarded, in an apathetic way, as a touchstone of nationality. The Gaelicisation policy was still regarded as an essential of national orthodoxy, dangerous to question publicly. The beauty and nobility of Gaeltacht landscape, and the romantic simplicity and immemorial quality of Gaeltacht lives, still pulled at the hearts of Irish people, who encountered them, if at all, in summer excursions and a mood of holiday receptivity.

Thus, ironically, the type of contradiction in Irish attitudes which Hyde had excoriated in 1892 was discernible once more, in novel form. He had pointed in 1892 to the illogicality of practical anglicisation being accompanied by undiminished anglophobia, and to the schizophrenic consequences, for Irish people, of attempting to serve two warring masters at once. A similar critic of 1942, fifty years on, might have relished the contradiction between the general acceptance in daily life of the continued supremacy of the English language, and the increased influence of British social modes in Ireland, and the constant, virtually unchallenged expenditure of Irish resources of many kinds in a patently hopeless battle to remove them.

Yet the great majority of Irish people lived as comfortably with the contradictions of 1942 as they had lived with the contradictions of 1892. To extend Adam Smith's dictum, there is a deal of anomaly, as well as ruin, in a nation; and children, as well as old men, forget. It is difficult to guess at the eventual state of mind of the cohorts which emerged from the 'Gaelicised' schooling system. But we can pretty confidently infer from the continued general sluggishness that it had provoked neither resentment nor enthusiasm, in any great degree, among the pupils. Probably the majority were confirmed in obeisance to the state policy by their school experience. Perhaps corporal punishment or Latin grammar may constitute a fair analogy. It is notorious that many who have groaned under these impositions in the classroom regard them with increasing favour as time heals the wounds, and come at last to see them as furnishing some social or intellectual advantage. So it may well have been with Irish, as compulsory. To have endured and survived it oneself may have been, if anything, an added reason for complacency when one's children were called upon to run the same course. With school behind them, the former pupils could, like the bulk of their elders in the population, leave it to others (the battle-hardened teachers and the raw child-recruits) to carry on the struggle.

There was of course one other body charged with the task of national regeneration, the hundred thousand (or fewer) native-speaking inhabitants of the Gaeltachts. Blythe's early schemes, largely confirmed by the Gaeltacht Commission of 1925, had cast them in the dual roles of custodians and evangelists of the native culture. It was also to be widely felt that, as (in the grandiloquent contemporary phrase) 'the Evicted Tenants of Our Race', they were owed a debt of honour by the remainder of the nation. On both counts, their little surviving territories were to be protected and fostered by infusions of state capital and the establishment of cottage industry. They were also to be extended by the compulsory purchase of non-Gaeltacht land on which some might be resettled. Meanwhile, the younger generation was to be favoured in recruitment to the teaching profession, the army, the police and the civil service and in entry to the universities.

It was a wild innumerate dream. Even the numerous Gaeltacht secondary schools and preparatory colleges planned to fit Gaeltacht children for higher education and a middle-class destiny could not possibly have been filled. Not only were there insufficient children in all, but also the hereditary education patterns of Gaeltacht people were quite foreign to the proposed crash programme. Almost all parents in the Gaeltachts wished to remove their children from school at the age of 12 years. It was only with difficulty that a handful could be persuaded to remain even to the age of 14; and further schooling was practically unknown. Yet it was this small and quite unready pool of children that was to supply, almost instantly, many hundreds of teachers and Gardai and a battalion of the army, to say nothing of the numbers needed by the grand design to fill civil service and university places. Moreover, it was inevitable that such drastic 'positive discrimination' in favour of native speakers, especially in the needy years between the wars, should have been resisted by the many who were being discriminated against. It was the opportunity for *state* employment (magical in the eyes of the Irish lower-middle and small-farming classes for being 'permanent and pensionable') which would be severely curtailed, if the Blythe policy were even half-realised.

Correspondingly, the proposed physical expansion of the Gaeltachts by land purchase clashed with the demands of the great body of the Irish rural poor for the creation or extension of small holdings for themselves.

Thus, it is not surprising that the Gaeltacht programme made little headway. It was unrealistic in its estimate of the capacity of the Irish-speaking population to spread across the land and into an extraordinary variety of unfamiliar occupations. It was unrealistic in its estimate of the willingness of the remainder of the Irish people to forgo jobs and incomes in pursuit of 'the national goal'. It was no less unrealistic (or self-deceiving) in forgetting that the 'Evicted Tenants of Our Race' wanted, as ever, their children to acquire the English language so that they might improve their material lot (probably by emigration overseas). Nor was it remembered that the folk culture of the western seaboard, however beautiful, was inextricably interwoven with a way of life which was, as Miss O'Callaghan has observed, cruelly hard and poor.

VI

By the time that Fianna Fail attained power in 1932 the Gaelicisation campaign had settled into a form of indeterminate trench warfare. Of course, Fianna Fail had proclaimed itself from its beginning, in 1926, to be *the* party of the restoration of the native language; and this was indisputably de Valera's second *idée fixe*. But even if 'me-moreism' was implied in the electoral programmes, it was difficult to advance beyond 'me-tooism' once in office. Cumann na nGael had left little unattempted along the lines of compulsion and direct *douceurs*. None the less, Fianna Fail managed to add something to the pressure upon the schools to Gaelicise, mainly because Thomas Derrig, its Minister of Education from 1932 to 1948 (with one nine-month interruption), and the leading members of the department during his regime, were merciless zealots, not to add unscrupulous bigots in the cause.

When the teachers complained formally in 1934 that compulsory Irish, in its current form, was impoverishing primary education, Derrig countered with a complaint that they were not advancing Gaelic as they should. He and his officers proceeded to *reduce* the teaching time available for English, mathematics and rural science, in the interests of speeding the campaign. They also formulated regulations *obliging* teachers with certificates of special competence in teaching through Irish (which carried a small reward) to do so, whatever the teachers' judgement of their pupils' capacity to learn by this procedure. The totalitarian strain now uppermost in the official ring of Gaelicisers manifested itself most clearly of all in the 'almost hysterical' [22] resistance of the minister and the department to every effort to launch an inquiry or investigation into the effects of their policy upon schools or children. Similarly, they (and the Gaelic League) denounced the mild and painfully moderate teachers' report of 1941 as anti-national and propagandist, and traduced its authors. The Derrig era probably revealed the Gaelic state of mind in its most ruthless, righteous and authoritarian form. But these tendencies had been apparent before the Gaelic League was 10 years old, and they were long to outlive the ferocious minister and his *apparatchiks*. Derrig-ism did not die in 1948. Derrig's successor was no less than Mulcahy. For that matter, none other than de Valera himself had substituted for him as Minister for Education in 1939. Not until the middle 1960s was there even an apparent modification in state policy towards the revival; and even thereafter the conduct of the Gaelgeoirs, ecclesiastical and lay alike, towards, for example, the Language Freedom Movement made it clear that the intolerance of opposition, which the INTO had encoun-tered in the 1930s, rankly flourished still.

The first half-century of official Gaelicisation had left Irish minds in a strange condition. The disposition of the zealots was, of course, complex only in the sense in which an amalgam of righteousness and coercion on the part of a minority invites some explanation. None will, however, be proferred here, beyond pointing to the familiarity of this phenomenen in nineteenth-century European history: Sabbatarians and secularists, chauvinists and socialist internationalists, Russificators and Prussian-isers, all, at one time or in one place or other, projected their fears on to another and defined themselves in terms of what they hated. Conversely, ex-Unionists in the Irish Free State fastened on Gaelicisation (together with prohibitory contraceptive and divorce legislation) as an oppressive symbol. It both manifested and, in their eyes, justified their self-chosen alienation from the new state in the first generation after independence. Here was a double irony. The Protestant Gaelicisers of the nineteenth century had set out to free Ireland of its exclusive associations with both the Catholic religion and social inferiority or degradation. Now the great majority of southern Irish Protestants linked it positively with the Cath-olic threat to their corporate survival, while they, together with their Catholic imitators, used 'improficiency' in 'the language' as an emblem of their superior social standing. According to their tacit doctrine, Gaelicism connoted the lower-middle classes and pressing upstarts, and vulgarity in general.

Simple partisanship was, however, impracticable for the bulk of Irish people. A condition of semi-Gaelicisation had settled down upon the country, while leaving large tracts of ordinary life untouched. It was quite possible for most adults to go from one year's end to the next without reading more Irish than they might find upon direction posts or at the top and tail of a communication from a government department. On the other hand, they could not but be aware that Irish was inter-mittently important in the public and quasi-public sectors. Especially was this the case with recruitment or qualification, even outside the range of the civil service proper or the teaching profession. For example, a county engineer might be appointed who was not the first, second or even third choice as an engineer, but who was adjudged the best of those who had passed the Gaelic test; or the field for a university chair in, say, Irish history might be effectively restricted to those who could demonstrate their ability to lecture in 'the language' – although, in either case, Irish might never be used in the actual course of the employment of the successful candidate. Correspondingly, all undergraduates of the National University had to pass an oral examination in Irish before they could proceed to their degrees; all Bar students had to prove their capacity to cross-examine in Irish before they could be called; and so on.

Now all this complicated one's state of mind. The principle of recruitment or advancement by merit was qualified, in various occupations, as closed competition replaced open; or, if one wishes, as another form of merit was taken to override the single measurement of professional ability. It was a further complication that the wind was sometimes tempered to the shorn lambs. Even bureaucracies have their secrets; but doubtless 'competence' in the language was not so inelastic an affair as 'always' to prevent desirable yet not effortlessly fluent candidates for office being appointed. Moreover, vernacular Irish as a qualification for entry to a degree or profession was often a near-empty form. Ultimate, if not immediate, failure for want of spoken facility was practically unknown. Sooner or later, every undergraduate proceeded to his degree; sooner or later, every Bar student received the call. Thus another type of nineteenth-century 'reform', rationalisation, was also partially reversed. Nothing smacked more of the *ancien régime* than ritualistic examination which debarred no one.

All this constituted a further layer of unreality to add to unrealism of the educational and Gaeltacht policies (in terms of their stated objectives) and of the official orthodoxy that the Gaelic language expressed, and was the chief distinguishing mark of the Irish national identity – and not just for the 'liberated' counties, but for the entire island, too. Once again, it does not necessarily follow that the bulk of Irish people felt at all uncomfortable in making obeisance to contradictory ideals or defying the evidence of their own experience. In fact, they either acquiesced in the Gaelicisation programme and its practical concomitants or at least did not find their inequity, capriciousness and irrationality grievous enough to warrant a concerted opposition. In short, like most other nations, they were willing to pay a moderate social price and, almost with eyes wide open, to deceive themselves in return for certain sentimental or emotional (but not therefore insignificant) satisfactions. Their state of mind upon the point may have been neither clear nor honest. But it did allow them to evade some disagreeable choices. Until – if ever – the day dawns when a junction of Northern Ireland and the Republic is seriously attempted, this sort of systematic ambivalence will doubtless continue to run its comparatively costless course.

Chapter 8

England's Opportunism,
Ireland's Difficulty

I

Down to 1922 political change in all parts of Ireland was, to a considerable extent, contingent upon British states of mind. Of course, these states of mind, in so far as they bore upon Ireland, were deeply influenced by current Irish happenings and campaigns. But they were by no means the simple product of such events or pressures. The self-images of Britons, the context of Empire and domestic party conflict at Westminster, all contributed some measure of separateness or autonomy to Britain's Irish policies. Hence, as we have noted earlier, the Irish difficulty in reading British signals. It was necessary to place them in an extra-Irish as well as in an Irish frame of reference if they were to be fully understood. The hoary Sellar and Yeatman joke that the trouble with the Irish Question was not that the English did not know the answer, but that the Irish kept changing the question, points to one element of the discordance. Generally it took much time for Britain to set aside the internal interests or extraneous preoccupations which distorted her apprehension of Irish realities. Sometimes, the delay was fatal to her own purpose; and tardy action was often followed by relapse.

Many leading events in Anglo-Irish relations exemplify this theme. The Ecclesiastical Titles Act of 1851 assuaged an outbreak of 'no popery' in Great Britain. The refusal to protect agriculture in the United Kingdom in 1879 satisfied the supposed need of Britain's urban population for cheap food. Both actions were taken without concern for their effects on Ireland. Yet each changed profoundly the shape and character of even *internal* Irish politics. Perhaps the clearest case in point, under the Act of Union, was the British decision of April 1918 to render Ireland liable to military conscription. The step was taken, in the teeth of all Irish advice, to appease various congeries of British discontent. Yet while its effects upon Britain were trivial, those upon Ireland were momentous. De Valera was established, at a bound, at the head of a national front; and the final supersession of the Irish Parliamentary Party by Sinn Fein was virtually assured. But it is probably more revealing to illustrate British distortion of Ireland's course of development by a comparison of complex historical sequences than by single episodes. This chapter will be devoted to one such comparison. I have selected for special examination the 'reflections' between the decade 1965–75 in Northern Ireland and the last two decades before the Act of Union in Ireland generally.

Such an exercise is 'reflective', not in the sense of Olympian rumination, but simply as images are seen in mirrors. Of course, the discovery of repetitive patterns in history is always a dangerous affair. Facts may be pressed to make the fit neater; the idiosyncracy of the past moment may drop out of sight; the propensity to see 'matches' in the respective series of events creeps upon one imperceptibly. For all that, it is worth attempting; in fact, it is always being attempted, whether consciously or unconsciously, by historians. After all, what is history but a dialogue between present apprehensions and knowledge of what has gone before? For historians, present and past are (to change the reflective metaphor) a pair of burning glasses. Angled rightly, they can light up designs or motifs in one another which may suddenly heighten our perception of each process. More particularly, the deeper tendencies in near-contemporary happenings, which are hard to discern in the babble and confusion of the moment, may be revealed quite clearly by examining a distant prototype, which has been considered coolly by scholars for generations.

II

The best historical illumination of Britain's conduct in Ireland in the late 1960s and early 1970s seems to me to lie (as I have implied already) in the era of 'Grattan's Parliament', that is to say, in the years between the formal liberation of the Irish Parliament from the control of Westminster and the British Privy Council in 1782 and its total eclipse by the Act of Union in 1801. The illumination is in many respects one of opposites – as indeed it is fitting when one talks of mirror images. Nor is this surprising. For, in very broad terms, the years of 'Grattan's Parliament' represented a stage of imperial aggrandisement by Great Britain (reluctant aggrandisement though it may have been), while the present represents a stage of hoped-for disengagement. None the less, whether reversed or plain, the correspondences between the two eras are uncannily numerous and close; and a leading reason for this fact would seem to be the constancy of British dispositions and mentalities, and the power which these can exercise upon Britain's political dependencies.

From the mid-1770s onwards, the view that Anglo-Irish relations were moving to a desperate crisis gained ground in the British governing circles. The success of the revolt of the American colonies and the concurrent achievements – or apparent achievements – of the Irish Volunteers in 1782 added to the sense of instability. But it was not produced by these developments. Well before they had taken place, men were putting two decades or even less as the limit in time to the maintenance of the system of indirect rule (whether through 'under-takers', the Irish equivalents of native paramount chiefs, or resident English viceroys) by which Ireland was controlled. As early as 1761 the prophecy was being made that if Ireland kept to her current course, either separation from or union with Great Britain would soon become an inescapable choice. What were the fundamental, the deep, reasons for this growing feeling that the rapids were near, that some horrendous climax was impending? Three would seem to deserve special emphasis.

The first of these reasons, I suggest, was the apparently irresistible onflow of religious toleration. Since 1691, to put it no earlier, British political control of Ireland had rested ultimately upon religious discrimination. It was their dependence upon British power for their engrossment of property and privilege which had made the British connection seem indispensable to the bulk of Irish Protestants. It did not matter if the Protestants were recent converts from Catholicism, as was increasingly the case after 1740. This merely created a broader and stronger base for privilege. It might matter significantly if the Protestants were Presbyterians, because in terms of privilege Irish Presbyterians faced both ways, degraded before Anglicans, but degrading Catholics; and it was a very serious question in which direction they would move, whenever a decision was forced upon them. But it unquestionably did matter critically if the area of Protestant privilege in Ireland was reduced or if the British will to enforce the exclusive system slackened; and the contemporary currents of toleration and indifferentism seemed likely to result in both developments. Hence, with the weakening of Protestant, and in particular Anglican, Ascendancy seeming, to the enlightened of the 1780s, part of a general European process, the traditional methods of British domination in Ireland were thrown into uncertainty.

A second, overlapping factor, not as yet clearly perceived but gradually becoming apparent, was the rise of a Catholic and the consolidation of a Presbyterian middle class in Ireland. A Catholic aristocracy and landed gentry had survived, where either luck or compliant Protestant relatives or friends had come to the rescue. If, for example, their leases happened to predate the popery laws of the 1690s, or an Anglican cousin allowed his name to be used in the land-title, a Catholic landowning family might hold on, even for several generations. But the steady pressure of the penal code had greatly reduced the number of these families. By 1750 they probably constituted less than 3 per cent of the proprietors. On the other hand, Catholics, gentle and common alike, had turned towards commerce. In particular, they had turned, in large numbers and with many individual instances of success, to the export trades to the continent and to retail trade at home. They exhibited moreover the classic characteristics of Protestant Nonconformist capitalism – frugality, the ploughing back of profits, the network of cousin-hoods providing investment capital, the modest, withdrawn style of life, and an alternative educational system – in this case furnished by the Anglo-Irish seminaries in France, Italy and Spain. Correspondingly, just as Catholics were driven into certain forms of commerce because of their exclusion from the guilds, so they were driven into certain professions or quasi-professions because they had been excluded from the remainder since the 1690s. Thus, for example, when barred from law, Catholics turned in large numbers to medicine. They may even have predominated numerically in this field – or at any rate in its lower ranges – after 1760.

As early as 1718 Archbishop King had observed that 'the Papists . . . already engrossed almost all the trade of the Kingdom'.[1] By the last quarter of the eighteenth century, the cumulative effect of sixty years of social and economic climbing and exertion had produced three important effects. First, the Catholic middle classes possessed, collectively, considerable wealth. John Keogh's claim in 1792 that nine-tenths of the personal wealth of Ireland was in Catholic hands was patently an exaggeration. But Keogh did have a very wide experience of Irish commerce; he was not talking wildly. Secondly, Catholics constituted, more and more, a creditor class, and Anglicans a debtor. The Ascendancy habitually overspent, in part, in keeping up with English Joneses, who possessed much greater initial resources; whose business habits were generally superior; and who regularly refreshed their order with huge infusions of commercial wealth from heiresses or entrepreneurial activity. Thirdly, the level of cultivation among the Catholic bourgeoisie, in intellectual, political and literary terms, had so risen that many were now on quite an equal footing with their Anglican counterparts. All three of these observations apply – the first two in an appropriately muted degree, and the third *a fortiori* – to the Irish Presbyterians of the north. The discriminations against the Presbyterians were but partial, and their way to the top was much shorter and less arduous. None the less, they reflected, even if palely, something of the Catholic plight and a great deal of the Catholic progress.

These developments were not seen distinctly or measured precisely in the Ireland of the 1770s and 1780s; still less so in England, one need hardly add. But there was, even in England, a gradual awakening to the general tendency of things. As this appreciation spread, it of course contributed to the growing sense that Ireland was insecure. Anglican power – the surrogate of British power – in Ireland rested upon an exclusive, or at least preponderating possession of wealth and education, as well as of force and office. The new developments were undermining the Anglican position, in so far as it rested on a monopoly of wealth, learning and sophistication; and this would surely produce a very dangerous instability in time.

The third fundamental reason why men in the late eighteenth century felt that a crisis in Anglo-Irish relations was imminent was that political, and particularly parliamentary, reform also seemed very close at hand. The spirit of the age may not have breathed out the idea of fundamental change in Britain. But it certainly did suggest that a more rational, uniform and comprehensive basis for the parliamentary system could not be staved off for long. But after 1782 British power in Ireland depended, mechanically speaking, not merely upon parliamentary abuses and corruption, but even, as the course of events in the 1790s showed, upon the systematic extension of such malpractices. There was no other means of ensuring parliamentary majorities in Ireland, and without sure majorities in the Irish House of Commons there was no guarantee that British policies, even in essentials, would prevail. Moreover, the American precedent of the 1770s and the general European phenomenon of burgher and aristocratic revolt in the 1780s suggested that trustee or vicarious government was tottering everywhere. In Ireland, it seemed, no more than a modest measure of parliamentary reform might be needed to throw off British parliamentary control, and to win self-determination for the Ascendancy, a body at once colonial, privileged and oligarchic.

It was in all these changing circumstances, and subject to all these political apprehensions, that the British government used its power in Ireland to force through relaxations of the anti-Catholic penal code. The first concessions, in 1778, enabling Catholics to lease, buy and bequeath land in specified areas, to resist conforming eldest sons, and to live in certain towns where they had hitherto been forbidden to reside, did not originate in London. But they were taken up warmly by Lord North and his Cabinet, and depended on British support and pressure for their passage. The rounding off of the 1778 Act in 1782 was acquiesced in rather than demanded by Westminster. But the crucial Relief Act of 1792, which repealed various obsolete provisions in the penal code and granted Catholics the right to practise law, was essentially Pitt's doing. The motivation of the British ministers from 1778 onwards was doubtless mixed. It may have been, in part, altruistic and humane; in part, an attempt to create an indigenous counterpoise to the Protestant monopoly in Ireland, and in part, an effort at neutralising, by partial appeasement, the potentially dangerous force of resurgent Catholicism. Whatever the relative weight of these three factors in the minds of North and Pitt and their respective colleagues, the last was certainly not least.

The point of no return in the checkmating process was reached in 1793 when the British Cabinet insisted upon the enfranchisement of Irish Catholics including the large body of Catholic 40s freeholders. War with France had both accentuated the importance of control of Ireland, and placed the papacy in the same camp as Britain, equal enemies of the Revolution. At the same time, the move helped to counteract the pressure for Irish parliamentary reform, by rendering the maintenance of the Protestant Ascendancy in Ireland less certain should the political ties with Great Britain ever loosen. Conversely, the predominant desires among the Irish Ascendancy in 1792–3 were to refuse the franchise to all Catholics and to press for such changes in the parliamentary system as might weaken British influence in the Irish House of Commons in their own collective interest. But they could not hold their ground against a determined Pitt.

Though with various checks and retreats, British policy proceeded in the same general direction until 1794–5, with the contrapuntal theme of Catholic and other reforms requiring an obdurate stand on, and an actual increase in, political abuses. Then came the hour of final decision. The reconstituted and ostensibly more liberal British government of 1794, produced by the adhesion of the Portland Whigs, seemed on the brink (however it jibbed and shivered) of compelling the Irish Parliament to pass a measure of Catholic Emancipation substantially like that of 1829. Pitt at the very last drew back. When the final calculations had to be made – and they could not be made coolly in the crisis precipitated by the new Whig Lord-Lieutenant, Fitzwilliam, who had immediately dismissed ultra-Protestants from the Irish government, and enflamed Catholic hopes – the risks appeared too great. It was not that emancipation would have threatened any immediate danger to the status quo. At most, it would have involved the entry of two or three dozen of the Catholic gentry, probably more servile than their Protestant brethren, to the Irish Parliament. As Canning put it mockingly thirty years later:

Suppose that . . . five or six Catholic gentlemen are admitted into parliament. The new comers would be, at first, I dare say, objects . . . of cautious and circumspect avoidance. They would have some inquisitive glances to encounter; and some doubts would be excited, and, perhaps, some wagers laid, as to their capacity to use the organs of ratiocination like less superstitious men. . . . But all this strangeness would wear off. In the course of a session or two we should venture upon a nearer approach; first, in little knots of two or three – taking care always to preserve a majority, – at last, perhaps, when we grew bolder, alone. Nay, the time would come when we should actually manage to sit beside them, with as much ease as we now manage to sit beside Unitarians – of whom we think more favourably only because they believe less than we do, whereas the Roman Catholics believe more.[2]

A handful of Catholics, within such a representative system as Ireland's in the 1790s, should certainly have caused no alarm. But it was impossible for any British statesman of foresight to suppose that indirect rule through parliamentary corruption could be maintained indefinitely. This being so, Catholic Emancipation might open a door which could not be closed at convenience. The fatal difficulty was that the 40s freeholders had been enfranchised already in 1793. When Emancipation was eventually yielded twenty-nine years after the Act of Union, it was in fact accompanied by their disfranchisement. But so heroic a reactionary step did not seem practicable – in fact, it occurred to nobody – within two years of the original concession. Nor did the British Cabinet in 1795 place much reliance on the lasting effects of conciliating the subjected. Gratitude, the humble Catholic gratitude which Pitt heard so much about, was a thing of the hour in politics – and even Catholic humility was wearing thin. The rising generation of Catholic laymen was no longer petitioning timidly for relief but rather demanding the instant removal of every legal discrimination. Thus, if the British government yielded even a little ground on Irish parliamentary reform, the Catholics might well secure some measure of independent political power – and that even without members of parliament of their own persuasion. This might, of course, be held *in terrorem* over the Irish Protestant Ascendancy by the British government. But it might equally be held *in terrorem* over Britain's interests in her dependency. Elements in Irish Protestantism might later, in resentment at their 'betrayal' by Great Britain or to secure some extra-sectarian objectives, make common cause with the enfranchised Catholics. Again, there was the British dimension to be considered. Anti-popery was once more a rising force in England. In this respect George III was rather a harbinger of the near future than an anachronistic bigot. As if his own intransigence were not enough, it was probably the case that he reflected British opinion in this field more accurately than did his Cabinet.

Finally, the Irish executive, dominated by the Lord Chancellor Fitzgibbon (whose father like many other Catholics of the mid-eighteenth century had conformed to the Established Church so that he might practise at the bar) was fiercely opposed to the concession. This was peculiarly important because the aid of the executive, and especially that of the juggernaut Fitzgibbon, was indispensable if an Act of Union were ever to be carried in Dublin – and already Pitt strongly favoured such an amalgamation. Three years before, when the Irish Ascendancy was struggling against the concession of the franchise to Catholics, he had written,

> The idea of the present fermentation gradually bringing both parties to think of an union with this country has long been in my mind. I hardly dare flatter myself with the hope of its taking place, but I believe it . . . to be the only solution for other and greater difficulties.[3]

Moreover Fitzgibbon's bold and cynical analysis of the Irish power struggle seemed all too convincing to busy, hard-headed politicians who knew Ireland only from the outside and were therefore susceptible to simplicity – Fitzgibbon himself had once observed that British statesmen were more ignorant of the affairs of Ireland than of any other country in the world. Fitzgibbon insisted that the Irish Protestant community was a beleaguered garrison which had seized, and held, its privileges by force. British arms sustained them in Ireland; nothing else could. They sustained British authority in Ireland; nothing else could. Beneath all the fine sentiments, fair words and temporary conjunctions of the day, this was the stark and eternal reality; and the choice facing the British government was either to maintain the Irish Protestant Ascendancy in power, place and property (which by now, he added, also implied a political union with Great Britain), or else to lose the island. There were of course immediate factors influencing the volte-face of Pitt and his ministry in 1795 – lobbying by expelled and threatened Irish placemen, Cabinet factionalism, George III's iron stupidity. There always are immediate factors. But it is the deeper causes and the long historical reasoning which concern us here.

The year 1795, therefore, marked the turning-point in British policy. At least, the strategic end of that policy, political control of Ireland, was henceforward sought by other means. Immediately, the moves towards parity for Catholics were halted. Later in the year, the failure to use governmental power to shield them from Orange aggression in Armagh, Down and Tyrone, or to amend the Insurrection Bill so as to deal equally with Catholic Defender and Orange disturbances in the north of Ireland, capped Fitzwilliam's recall. All this precipitated a cycle of violence and repression, which involved in turn Presbyterian and Catholic conflict, Presbyterian and Anglican rapport, changes in the mass support of the United Irish movement from Presbyterian to Catholic, and finally the Wexford outbreak of 1798. One development of 1796–7 deserves special notice. What 'added greatly', Lecky observes, 'to the anarchy of the North and had ultimately a most serious influence on the remainder of Ireland, was the growing importance of the Orange movement, and the alliance which was gradually forming between it and the Government'.[4] At first Orangeism was little more than what a contemporary termed 'the Protestant side of a faction fight'. Essentially it was the successor of Protestant Whiteboyism. But as the United Irishmen penetrated more and more deeply into the ranks of the Catholic peasantry and intermeshed more and more with their agrarian societies in 1796 and 1797, the Protestant gentry in Ulster assumed command of the Orange movement, and their Protestant tenants and labourers were recruited to fill the ranks of the repressive yeomanry and militia. Over Ireland as a whole, the power and authority of the state were being ranged against the larger sect by and through the fear-ridden minority.

All this did not mean, however, that the British government determined in 1795 or in any later year to throw its weight *permanently* behind unremitting Protestant Ascendancy, constant Catholic abasement and a pocket Parliament. None of these seemed durable in the long run. Nor indeed did the government rate the Irish Protestants *per se* much higher than Irish Catholics. Westmorland, Fitzwilliam's predecessor as Lord-Lieutenant, had told Pitt that as the Irish Protestants swore that even a union would be preferable to equality with Catholics, while the Catholics swore that even a union would be preferable to their continued degradation, 'the violence of both parties might be turned on this occasion to the advantage of England'.[5] If, he added, 'the Protestants should get over their Catholic prejudices, adieu to that cure [a union] for this country; however, I do not think that very likely'.[6] A union which would convert a large Catholic majority in Ireland into a minority of 20 per cent at most in a new United Kingdom, which would cut back forever the pretensions of the Ascendancy, which would moreover obviate the necessity for maintaining, with ever-increasing difficulty, a scandalous and precarious parliamentary order in Dublin – such a union seemed more than ever attractive in London's eyes.

The bloody rebellion of 1798 clinched the entire affair. An Irish Protestant front now clearly emerged, with security for Protestant lives, interests and property as its overriding object. Fitzgibbon's argument, that such security could be found only in a union with Great Britain, was making rapid advances in the upper circles of the Irish Ascendancy. At the same time, it would be as dangerous (from Britain's standpoint) to endorse blindly and for the indefinite future the actions of this frightened faction as to crush every hope of further amelioration in Catholic breasts. So the die was cast. Union, coupled with Catholic Emancipation and supra-factional government, was determined on. But union, when it came, was coupled with other and very different things – the maintenance of the old Ascendancy, intact; the rejection of the Catholic claims for parity; and the retention of the old Irish executive, unrepentant. Political ineptitude and cowardice, ill-fortune and unexhausted bigotry, succeeded at the very end in turning Britain's Irish tactics inside out.

III

Clearly, Britain's Irish policy in 1780–1801 had not been consistent. True, there were two constants: an ever-growing fear that political control of Ireland was in danger, and a gradually crystallising belief that the only absolute security for that control was direct rule by means of a union of the kingdoms. But beneath these grand, general concepts there was much backing and filling as to which line of action to adopt, and whom to conciliate, and to what degree. The explanation of the frequent, and occasionally drastic and fateful, changes of direction which followed lies, in part, in British domestic politics, in part in Britain's foreign policies and, in part, in the advice from Ireland which the British Cabinets happened to listen to from time to time. But it also lies, in part, in plain inattention to Ireland's problems, in particular phases or at particular junctures.

This last could be the critical factor. We might well name it the negative face of opportunism. If the Act of Union itself exemplified English opportunism in the obvious sense – that advantage was taken of the alarm produced by the rising of 1798 to carry through a predetermined measure – the Act's immediate aftermath exemplified English opportunism of the second sort. In 1801–4 Ireland was politically torpid. To an unusual degree, it was practicable for the British Cabinet to shelve her problems; and the blessed opportunity for inertia was not lost. But inattention to Ireland's problems in the very years in which the practical meaning of the Union was being determined proved important. It helps to explain why Ireland failed to follow the integrative course of Scotland after 1707 but remained instead under a viceregal system. It helps to explain why the *raison d'être* of the Union of 1801 – the nullifying of the Irish Catholic threat by concessions which would be 'safe' when this body became a relatively small minority – dropped out of sight. Most telling of all, it helps to explain why no move towards power-sharing or office-sharing between Irish Protestants and Catholics was attempted. Britain was to reap a grim harvest in the 1820s and 1830s for these three interlocked neglects. Yet they were wholly the consequence of her own 'un-policy' at a point when Anglo-Irish relations were at once extraordinarily plastic and extraordinarily undemanding.

IV

Before we try to compare all this to the current conflict in Northern Ireland, the distant stage-setting for that conflict is worth consideration. The treaty negotiations of 1921 and their aftermath bear certain general resemblances to the Act of Union and its sequel. Great Britain's ultimate objectives in the 1921 negotiations were to keep Ireland within the empire, and to maintain the system of imperial defence intact. The fate of the Ulster Protestants was a secondary concern. They would probably have been subjected in November 1921 to heavy British pressure to enter some form or other of political union with the bulk of their fellow-countrymen had the negotiations – quite fortuitously so far as Northern Ireland was concerned – not taken some unexpected turns. Even in the Treaty itself, it can scarcely be doubted that the British signatories genuinely intended the Boundary Commission

as a lever to urge Craig and his colleagues [the Ulster Unionists] to accept an all-Ireland settlement. By Article 14 they were guaranteed that the Northern Parliament could continue to function, but it would be subordinate to the all-Ireland Parliament. But if they declined to

avail themselves of that offer, they must be prepared to lose a considerable part of the Six Counties.[7]

Lloyd George was well aware of how considerable a 'loss' the leading
Irish delegates anticipated. Collins had just told him that the commission
would 'save' Counties Fermanagh and Tyrone, and large parts of
Counties Armagh, Derry and Down for the Dublin parliament. Griffith
had earlier made it clear that his expectations were the same, apart from
certain comparatively small areas in Fermanagh and Tyrone with
decided Unionist majorities. Nor had the British signatories reason to
suppose that such anticipations were unrealistic. True, the criterion for
dividing Ulster had been altered. The phrase 'so far as may be compatible
with economic and geographic conditions' had been substituted for the
vaguer 'as closely as possible', to qualify the agreement that the border be
determined in accordance with the wishes of the inhabitants. But, in the
framing of this clause, the British as well as the Irish parties had probably
in mind merely the enclaves of Catholics far behind any likely border,
those in Belfast itself or northern Antrim, for example. No one on the
night of 5–6 December 1921, when the treaty was signed, would have
guessed that the provision would be interpreted as sanctioning the
interchange of a mere 232,000 acres and a mere 38,000 people in all.
Lloyd George himself expected that at least five times that area and at
least five times that number would be transferred to the Irish Free State.
After the treaty had been signed he told the House of Commons that
Counties Fermanagh and Tyrone would have to go to the southern state,
if Northern Ireland remained obdurate.

> Take it either by constituency or by Poor Law Union, or, if you like,
> by counting heads, and you will find that the majority in these counties
> prefer to be with their Southern neighbours – What does this mean? If
> Ulster is to remain a separate community, you can only by means of
> coercion keep them there, and although I am against the coercion of
> Ulster, I do not believe in Ulster coercing other units.[8]

Thus in return for an oath of allegiance to the Crown, no larger
measure of independence than dominionhood for the Irish Free State,
and three naval bases, the British government was prepared to coerce
Northern Ireland into either some form of union with the remainder of
the island or the cession of (in all likelihood) something between 30 and
45 per cent of its total territory. It is difficult to say which alternative
would have served British interests better. But certainly either was
preferable for Great Britain – in the special sense of storing up less
trouble for the future – than the maintenance of the six counties of
Northern Ireland intact. This should have been clear to any farsighted
British statesman at the time.

But just as the rational corollary of the Act of Union in 1801 was abandoned once the pressure to act fell off, so too with the rational corollary to the Treaty of 1921. In 1922 and 1923 the government of the Irish Free State was preoccupied with the survival of the new regime in even twenty-six of the Irish counties. It was in no condition to badger Britain to institute the Boundary Commission immediately. Conversely, the government of Northern Ireland instantly took its stand upon the inviolability of the current boundary; and this implied mere inaction. Thus Britain enjoyed unwonted relief from major Irish difficulties in the immediate aftermath of the Treaty. She had ample difficulties of her own, with the postwar depression compounded by political travail. In the three general elections of 1922–4 (and to the accompaniment of successive minority governments), Labour was painfully replacing the Liberals as the second national party in a two-party state. In these circumstances it was all too easy for the British Cabinets to lose sight of the strategic ends of the 1921 settlement.

To the ordinary *vis inertiae* governing politicians who are not being chivvied (and especially so on an issue promising no electoral advantage), two other powerful forces were added. One was prescription. Borders take on a life of their own quite quickly. After even two and a half years people were habituated to the image of a divided Ireland. Each month, and each physical manifestation of political separation, augmented both the impression that the border had come about by deliberate choice, and the impression of its permanence. All this applied with special force to those without special knowledge of or special interest in Ireland. The second factor was the natural bias of Englishmen in favour of those who were racially kin, confessionally Protestant and noisily loyal to Crown and Empire. The sophisticated might speak of race, religion in politics, or the traditional symbols of allegiance as *passé*; but the warp of even the most 'sophisticated' English mind was in its own fashion nationalistic. It needed the magnet of present and pressing Irish troubles to pull it on to a true line of appraisal; and this magnet was practically inoperative in 1922. Thus, in the absence of Irish agitation, the appointment, the terms of reference and the composition of the Boundary Commission were carelessly, and even negligently, handled by the British Cabinets. Worse still, British signatories to the treaty such as Birkenhead and Austen Chamberlain began to prepare the way for minimal change by declaring that only minor 'rectifications' of the frontier had been intended when the commission was proposed. As with the Act of Union, British policy was in the end turned inside out because the customary British indifference and self-approval displaced the sharper awareness of Irish realities which the great crisis had temporarily produced.

V

It would be absurd to try to explain in any simple or literal fashion recent British policy in Ireland in terms of late-eighteenth-century history. Yet it is impossible, I believe, to think for long upon the two phases without a feeling of *déjà vu* sweeping over one repeatedly. Again and again, the strong lines of the early pattern seem to show through the later. So let us shake up and try to rearrange, in another temporal context, the pieces used in the first part of this chapter to establish the underlying historical design.

One critical element in the late-eighteenth-century situation was apparently reversed in the case of Northern Ireland after 1921. Instead of Protestants forming a small minority but engrossing an oligarchic parliamentary system, they now formed a considerable majority in a formally democratic polity. In the new state of Northern Ireland the Catholics constituted one-third of the total population, as against three-quarters in eighteenth-century Ireland. Such was actually the case, even if few Ulster Catholics accepted the arithmetic, because they still looked forward to the political reintegration of their island. It is also true that, unlike their eighteenth-century forefathers, the northern Catholics possessed substantial electoral rights, and suffered from few if any formal disabilities at law. Moreover, Stormont's relationship to Westminster between 1921 and 1972 was totally different, both on paper and in fact, from the relationship of College Green to Westminster between 1782 and 1800. Stormont, ostensibly a dependent assembly, was left largely to its own devices – down to 1968, at least. College Green, ostensibly an autonomous Parliament, was in practice carefully supervised and directed.

At the same time, we should not forget that all these are comparatively superficial distinctions in terms of our overriding interest. After all, Stormont was identical with the eighteenth-century Irish assembly in being 'a Protestant parliament for a Protestant people' – to employ the succinct description of its master-builder, Sir James Craig. Proportional representation in parliamentary elections was abandoned by the Ulster Unionists at the first possible opportunity. But this, contrary to the general belief, was done to consolidate the Protestant vote rather than to underrepresent the Catholic. Protestant splinter groups were seen as the prime danger to security; Catholic alienation did not matter. Similarly, the governing Unionist Party was wholly sectarian from the start; and the regional and district boundaries were drawn, often in a most inequitable fashion, to render its hegemony complete. The political system and local government, law and public order, industry and jobs, were so arranged and operated as to ensure an overwhelming predominance of power, pride, prospects and possession for the Protestant community. This was 'Grattan's Parliament' upside down, the Ascendancy of a multi-class majority. But the difference was essentially mechanical. The ultimate objective and achievement, Protestant supremacy, was just the same.

Here is an instance of the historical pattern reversed in detail, so to say, though repeating the general design. When we turn, however, to the three fundamental factors predisposing British politicians in the late eighteenth century to the Act of Union, we can find close analogues for each in the British attitudes to Northern Ireland after the Second World War. With the first of these, the effects of a general wave of rationalism and 'enlightenment' upon British public conduct, we can see in the mid-twentieth century a pattern which substantially duplicated the original form. The changes in and successes of European liberalism (or libertarianism, if one wishes) in the 1950s form a true counterpart to the rapid and wide diffusion of indifferentist humanism in the late eighteenth century. Two elements of the new enlightenment of the 1950s were of particular importance for the future of Northern Ireland. First, the idea that society might have a religious or sectarian basis became more and more alien, not so say incomprehensible, in Britain. Concurrently, the sense of a common Protestant interest, or of a Protestant 'family' divided but physically by the Irish Sea, dwindled almost to nothing. Secondly, with the consciousness of international decline, British nationalism became more strident and overt; and, as a sort of counterpoint, British racialism, as applied to those living outside Britain itself, grew ever fainter. Again the effect was to weaken the British sense of identity with and responsibility for Ulster Unionists. Thus in the 1960s, as in the 1780s, religion and the sense of kinship ceased to be the effective bonds, tying Great Britain and its outlying Irish 'possession'.

Similarly with the second major factor. Unlike the Irish Catholics of the middle decades of the eighteenth century, the northern Catholics of the middle decades of the twentieth did not throw up an extensive mercantile class. But outside forces did produce equivalent Catholic social and economic advances, with their attendant political problems. The Butler Education Act of 1944, the Beveridge reforms in the social services and the revolution in the British system of personal taxation during the war had, cumulatively and interactively, profound levelling tendencies in Northern Ireland – at any rate over a considerable period of time. By the 1960s much the same sort of disparity had opened up between northern Catholics' self-perception of their social worth and the actual places into which they were locked by the organised society, as had opened up for the Catholic middle classes in Ireland generally by the 1770s. Successive British governments, with British political objectives in view but legislating willy-nilly for the entire United Kingdom, had inadvertently altered the balances in Northern Ireland. They would soon be as abruptly confronted by the consequences of these gradual developments as their predecessors had been abruptly confronted, in the last quarter of the eighteenth century, by a Catholic bourgeoisie.

The third general factor presaging drastic change in Ireland from the 1770s onwards was the apparent onset of political reform in Britain, and the implications of this for her dependencies. Again, we can discern a close counterpart in the 1950s and 1960s. In the first case, it was primarily a matter of circumscribed parliamentary reform, of the extension and the independence of the small exclusive electorate. But in the second, the concept of civil rights was of course much broader. It had moved far and fast beyond mere legal and electoral equality to the idea of parity in terms of employment, housing, education and social opportunity in general. Once such ideas were abroad, and still more when notions of 'positive discrimination' began to make their appearance, the entire social arrangement of Northern Ireland was bound to appear curious in British eyes. Moreover, as Britain moved towards proclaiming the virtues of the new civil rights for what was euphemistically termed the New Commonwealth, the existence of large bodies of 'white coloureds' under her own direct jurisdiction appeared ever more awkward to explain, let alone to justify. The government of Northern Ireland itself was by no means unruffled, in the early 1960s, by the winds of change springing up across the Irish Sea. But when it drew British attention, continuously and upon a considerable scale, upon itself, 'Ulster' stood forth, anomalous and indefensible in its manifold discriminations and inequities, just as Ireland as a whole had done nearly two centuries before.

VI

To move, in turn, to comparative analysis, perhaps the closest point of resemblance, in Britain's Irish policy, between the last two decades of the eighteenth century and the decade 1965–75 in Ulster was the attempt to compensate for constitutional and political frustrations by egalitarian and eleemosynary reform. Readiness to put off intractable political problems by forcing a course of social and economic parity upon a reluctant Irish executive and Parliament is the essential mark of both phases. True, the train of concessions to Catholics from 1778 to 1795 did not depend entirely upon British power. It was aided, in the earlier stages at least, by a new spirit of toleration among considerable numbers of educated Irish Protestants, and by a temporary loosening of the Protestant front, which allowed a certain degree of open expression to the latent bourgeois–gentry and Presbyterian–Anglican antagonisms. But these Irish forces were mere assistants of the course of concession. They did not, they probably could not, have directed and forced it through alone. British pressure was the ultimate determinant.

Now, at quite a tolerable level of historical generalisation, the last four sentences, describing 1778–95, can be used, virtually unchanged, as an elementary analysis of the sequence of events in Northern Ireland in the years 1968–71. In each case, the political system, which operated to secure a near-monopoly of power and a great preponderance of office to the Protestant community, was left substantially intact. Instead, the attempt was made to circumvent the problem by, in terms of the Catholic community, killing self-rule by kindness. But in each case this attempt produced effects fatal to its own success among Irish Protestants. It aroused fears that a process of surrender under threat, a process of which no one knew the end or limit, had been set in motion. More, it was argued that such a step was fundamentally misconceived because it was notorious that Catholic appetites merely grew with feeding. Further still, it seemed to growing numbers in the privileged sects that the course of concession to the Catholics was manufacturing a formidable confessional separatist movement out of what had been up to then mere ancestral posturing and shibboleths. Again, the new British stance of towering above the Irish factions roused Ulster Protestants to a belief – or if one wishes the realisation – that they were at the mercy of forces at Westminster and Whitehall beyond their own control. This was a familiar feeling in Ireland, experienced at many times and by many parties; and in the north it was reinforced by the well-remembered traumas of 1911–14. As usual, apprehension, resentment, and campaigns to tip the balance of fear in London followed fast. For a second time, I suggest, the same general analysis may be applied, with almost equal force, to our respective time-divided phases.

Yet again we have matching outcomes of the stage of Protestant counter-pressure, and of growing alienation between the initially responsive Catholic body and the British government. Fitzwilliam's recall and the repression which it signalled seem to anticipate essentially, and in actual point of sequence, the institution of internment without trial, in the modern context. Did not August 1971 represent precisely the same type of policy reversal as 1795? In each case, a repolarisation of the Irish parties had been under way for some time before the denouement. In each case, violence had begun to manifest itself; arms were being gathered; and belligerent organisation had rapidly advanced. In each case, the British Cabinet moved back to its accustomed stand in such circumstances – that all processes of political change must be postponed until the danger to public order has been 'crushed' by 'firm measures'. This did not necessarily mean that the British Cabinet saw itself in 1795 or in 1971 as either partisan or opposed to further reform – although it was not without significance that, in both 1794 and late 1970, conservatives had suddenly gained ground in the policy-making coteries in London. But the flattering self-image of the British Cabinet and what it thought it intended for the future were clear different things from how its actions and intentions appeared in Ireland. The action taken was inevitably both partisan and thoroughly destructive in Irish terms. This was so because the existing machinery of control and suppression in Ireland was still, essentially, in the hands of one particular faction; because one special interest there was still, for all practical purposes, synonomous with the state; and because that special interest still named itself, and managed for the moment to persuade most Englishmen that it was in fact 'British'. For the third time, I suggest, a single outline of events fits quite as closely the twentieth-century as the eighteenth-century phase.

I shall venture one final turn of the screw. Does not the Act of Union of 1801, subsuming the Irish Parliament in the imperial, bear a true resemblance, in reverse, to the suspension of Stormont, the Parliament of Northern Ireland, in 1972? For although Northern Ireland attained 'Home Rule' in 1921, this did not happen because it was positively desired by any party. It happened because it seemed the most effective mode, in the circumstances of the day, of maintaining the Act of Union, substantially, in at least six of the thirty-two counties of Ireland. Thus, paradoxically, the inauguration of a system of indirect rule in Northern Ireland in 1921 really signified the confirmation of the British connection. By a corresponding paradox, the establishment of direct rule almost fifty-one years later really signified the weakening, and perhaps ultimately the dissolution, of the tie between Great Britain and 'Ulster'. It is true that, at the time, full political integration between the two was said to be one of the alternative future courses. But even at the moment of Stormont's suspension, this seemed improbable; and every later twist and turn of events in the north has rendered such an outcome still more unlikely. If this view of the significance of the suspension is right, then the remnant of the Act of Union, which had survived 1921, died or was placed under death sentence in March 1972; and in the history of the Act, 1972 is a date second only in import to 1801 or 1922 – in fact, the final entry in the ledger.

If this is true, if we are really speaking of the opening and the closing of a ledger, where then lie the counterparts of which I speak? For me they lie in 1801 and 1972 representing, equally, the clear end of one era in the Anglo-Irish relationship, accompanied by ambiguity as to the meaning of what had been done, and unpredictability as to what would follow. Perhaps the most striking single feature of the British preconsideration of both constitutional union in the 1790s and of the imposition of direct rule in the 1970s was absorption in the immediate. Each stroke was seen in terms of a current problem, in terms of breaking an impasse, of cutting a hopeless tangle. But whatever the tactical merits of the respective initiatives, each was undertaken without a really determined strategy. Of course, some large if hazy strategical notions accompanied both sets of tactics. As we have seen, Catholic equality and the full political integration of Ireland with Great Britain were in the minds of the ministers in 1800; just as, doubtless, some conception of shared power, such as that emerging from the Sunningdale Conference of 1973 – to form a climbing-frame for a new joint Ulster identity to develop – was in the minds of the ministers in 1971. But in practice these turned out to be scarcely more than an amalgam of Micawberism and the indestructible belief that, given sufficient time, pain and menaces, other peoples could be brought to the level of British reasonableness.

Let me give as one example of the fundamental irresponsibility – one is tempted to say frivolity – with which such great steps were taken, the matter of a separate Irish executive in and after 1801. The Act of Union was both on the statute book and in effect before the question, whether or not the Lord-Lieutenancy, and all the attendant apparatus of state, domestic power and patronage, would continue in Ireland, so much as crossed the mind of any member of a British Cabinet. The question never was determined in any serious sense – unless *vis inertiae* is serious. Thus, the Irish sub-state of the nineteenth century, so critical to the shape and development of the Irish question down to 1920, was never planned; it just never – so to say – unhappened. Correspondingly, the logical corollary of the establishment of a power-sharing assembly in Northern Ireland in 1974, as the first stage of British disengagement in Ulster, was to support that assembly by all the instruments of power in the hands of the British government. But this was immediately forgotten or foresworn at the first manifestation, within a few months of the inauguration of mixed local rule, of serious Ulster Protestant resistance to the experiment. The strategy of 1972 was never really put to the test. Once it encountered a major, though quite predictable, obstacle, in the so-called Ulster Workers' Council strike, British policy veered away in other directions, or rather into the familiar void. From being serious but never desperate, the Ulster question had, apparently, been reclassified in London as desperate, but never serious.

What have we then as the final mark of the great initiatives? A leap in the dark, a shooting of Niagara? Well, no, perhaps not; but, at least – to close each of the intolerable crises – the pushing of another in the dark, another shot insouciantly across the falls. A very different metaphor, that of impregnation, is used by Seamus Heaney in *Act of Union* to apostrophise the price which Ireland pays for ancient British drives and current British absences of mind or will. As the poem opens, the man, England, addresses the woman, Ireland, thus:

> Conquest is a lie. I grow older
> Conceding your half-independent shore
> Within whose borders now my legacy
> Culminates inexorably . . .
>
> And I am still imperially
> Male, leaving you with the pain,
> The rending process in the colony,
> The battering ram, the boom burst from within.

There is a dreadful constancy in being vulnerable.

References

Chapter 1

1 E. Holt, *Protest under Arms: The Irish Troubles, 1916–23* (London, 1960), p. 258.
2 *Parliamentary Register* (Ireland), vii, p. 500 (Sir Francis Hutchinson).
3 D. McCartney, 'The Writing of History in Ireland, 1800–1830', *Irish Historical Studies*, Vol. x, 1957, p. 358. I am much indebted to this article for information on early-nineteenth-century Irish historiography.
4 Meeting of Irishmen in New York (New York, 1825), pp. 9–11, quoted in ibid., p. 362.
5 W. Phelan, *The History of the Policy of the Church of Rome in Ireland* (London, 1827), quoted in ibid., p. 361.
6 M. O'Connell (ed.), *The Correspondence of Daniel O'Connell* (Dublin, 1974), Vol. iv, pp. 87–8.
7 E. Curtis and R. B. McDowell (eds), *Irish Historical Documents* (London, 1943), p. 314.
8 *Hansard*, 5th series, lviii, col. 174, 11 February 1914.
9 Curtis and McDowell (eds), *Documents*, p. 304.
10 M. O'Connell (ed.), *O'Connell Correspondence*, Vol. iii, p. 30.
11 H. M. Moran, *Viewless Winds: Being the Recollections and Digressions of an Australian Surgeon* (London, 1939), pp. 407–8.
12 Lady Trevelyan (ed.), *The Complete Works of Lord Macaulay* (London, 1875), Vol. i, p. 180.
13 J. W. Burrow, *A Liberal Descent* (London, 1981), p. 65.
14 Trevelyan (ed.), *Macaulay Works*, Vol. i, p. 327.
15 *Hansard*, 5th series, lxv, cols 1828–9, 3 August 1914. Redmond prefaced these remarks with, 'There is a possibility, at any rate, of history repeating itself'.
16 G. K. Chesterton, *Irish Impressions* (London, 1919), p. 72.

Chapter 2

1 *A Report on the Debate of the Irish Bar, Sunday the 9th December 1798, on the Subject of an Union of the Legislatures of Great Britain and Ireland* (Dublin, 1798). The anti-unionists triumphed by 166 to 32 votes.
2 R. Barry O'Brien (ed.), *The Autobiography of Theobald Wolfe Tone* (Dublin, n.d.), Vol. i, p. 26.
3 Thomas Wyse, *Historical Sketch of the Late Catholic Association of Ireland* (London, 1829), Vol. i, p. 401.
4 ibid., p. 405.
5 J. R. O'Flanagan, *Life and Times of Daniel O'Connell* (Dublin, 1875), p. 641.
6 *Hansard*, 5th series, xxxix, col. 1068, 13 June 1912.
7 S. Rosenbaum (ed.), *Against Home Rule: the Case for the Union* (London, 1912), p. 170.
8 J. O'Connell (ed.), *The Select Speeches of Daniel O'Connell M.P.* (Dublin, 1854), Vol. i, p. 9.
9 ibid., p. 20.
10 These quotations are drawn respectively from the stories 'Phillipa's Foxhunt' and 'The Finger of Mrs Knox'. See generally O. MacDonagh, *The Nineteenth Century Novel and Irish Social History: Some Aspects* (Dublin, 1970).
11 W. J. Fitzpatrick (ed.), *The Correspondence of Daniel O'Connell the Liberator* (London, 1888), Vol. ii, p. 152.

12 F. S. L. Lyons, 'The Minority Problem in the 26 Counties', in F. MacManus (ed.), *The Years of the Great Test* (Cork, 1967), pp. 99–100.
13 *Parliamentary History*, xxxiv, cols 747–8.
14 ibid., xxxv, cols 166–7. Sylvester Douglas had carried this argument further in the House of Commons by contrasting Britain's ready access to the continent with the fact that she was Ireland's 'only neighbour . . . Great Britain intercepts almost entirely all direct communication between Ireland and the continent of Europe, while the universal expanse of the Atlantic divides that island from all other parts of the globe', ibid., xxxiv, col. 851.
15 Rosenbaum (ed.), *Against Home Rule*, p. 135.

Chapter 3

1 A. V. Dicey, *Law and Public Opinion in England in the Nineteenth Century* (2nd edn: London, 1914), p. 41. See generally, O. MacDonagh, ' "Pre-transformations": Victorian Britain', in E. Kamenka and Alice E.-S. Tay (eds), *Law and Social Control* (London, 1980), on which this chapter draws to a considerable extent.
2 W. L. Burn, 'Free Trade in Land: an Aspect of the Irish Question', *Transactions of the Royal Historical Society*, 4th series, xxxi, 68.
3 23 & 24 Vic. c. 154, clause 3.
4 R. D. Collison Black, *Economic Thought and the Irish Question 1817–70* (Cambridge, 1960), p. 29.
5 Barbara Solow, 'A New Look at the Irish Land Question', *Economic and Social Review*, vol. xii, no. 4, p. 303.
6 M. O'Connell (ed.), *The Correspondence of Daniel O'Connell* (Dublin, 1974), Vol. ii, pp. 356–7.
7 Solow, 'Irish Land Question', p. 306.
8 W. E. Vaughan, 'An Assessment of the Economic Performance of Irish Landlords, 1851–81', in F. S. L. Lyons and R. A. J. Hawkins (eds), *Ireland under the Union: Varieties of Tension* (Oxford, 1980), p. 198.
9 *Hansard*, 3rd series, cxc, cols 1525–6, 16 March 1868.
10 T. Brown, *Ireland: a Social and Cultural History* (London, 1981), pp. 24–5.

Chapter 4

1 N. Mansergh, *The Irish Question* (London, 1965), p. 226.
2 *Quarterly Review*, cxxxiii, no. 266, October 1867, p. 572.
3 H. Begbie, *The Lady Next Door* (London, n.d.), p. 24.
4 *Nation*, 4 March 1843.
5 *Freeman's Journal*, 16 April 1840.
6 J. Levy (ed.), *A Full and Revised Report of the three days discussion in the Corporation of Dublin on the Repeal of the Union* . . . (Dublin, 1843), pp. 191–2.
7 R. Barry O'Brien, *The Life of Charles Stewart Parnell* (London, 1898) p. 3. On whether the words 'the last link' were actually used, or at any rate actually reported at the time, see F. S. L. Lyons, *Charles Stewart Parnell* (London, 1977), pp. 111–12.
8 *Freeman's Journal*, 11 December 1890.
9 Lyons, *Parnell*, p. 614.
10 *Nation*, 24 January 1885.
11 *Freeman's Journal*, 18 October 1882.
12 *Hansard*, 3rd series, ccciv, col. 1134, 8 April 1886.
13 R. P. Davis, *Arthur Griffith and Non-Violent Sinn Fein* (Dublin, 1974), p. xv. I am much indebted to this work for the information on Griffith which has been used in this section.

Chapter 5

1 T. Dunne, *Theobald Wolfe Tone, Colonial Outsider: an Analysis of his Political Philosophy* (Cork, 1982), p. 15.
2 *Historical Ballad Poetry of Ireland* (Dublin, 1910), p. 184. Although the author of this poem, Aubrey de Vere, was too young to be a member of the *Nation* 'group', his patriotic verse is fully representative of the *Nation* 'school'.
3 M. MacDonagh, *The Life of Daniel O'Connell* (London, 1903), p. 391.
4 J. O'Leary, *Recollections of Fenians and Fenianism* (London, 1896), Vol. i, p. 4.
5 *Nation*, 17 June 1843.
6 *Nation*, 1 August 1846.
7 *Nation*, 22 November 1845. Among the 'hints' offered in the editorial was, 'every railway within five miles of Dublin could in one night be totally cut off from the interior country. To lift a mile of rail, to fill a perch or two of any cutting or tunnel, to break down a piece of an embankment, seem obvious and easy enough.'
8 E. Abbott, *Historical Aspects of the Immigration Problem* (New York, 1924), p. 483.
9 O'Leary, *Fenians and Fenianism*, Vol. i, pp. 101–2.
10 J. Denieffe, *Personal Narrative of the Irish Revolutionary Brotherhood* (New York, 1906), Vol. 1, p. 25.
11 S. Pender, *Fenianism: a Centenary Lecture* (Cork, 1967), p. 5.
12 O'Leary, *Fenians and Fenianism*, Vol. i, p. 27.
13 ibid., p. 28.
14 *Collected Works of Padraic H. Pearse: Political Writings and Speeches* (Dublin, 1922), pp. 98–9.
15 ibid., p. 216.
16 Ruth Dudley Edwards, *Patrick Pearse: the Triumph of Failure* (London, 1977), p. 19. I am much indebted to this work for information on Pearse which has been used in this section.
17 *Pearse: Political Writings*, p. 37.
18 ibid., p. 226.
19 *An Barr Buadh*, 16 March 1912, quoted in Edwards, *Pearse: Triumph of Failure*, pp. 161–2.
20 J. Boswell, *The Journal of a Tour of the Hebrides with Samuel Johnson* (Everyman edn: London, 1958), p. 68.

Chapter 6

1 *Pilot*, 12 January 1835. See generally O. MacDonagh, 'The Politicization of the Irish Catholic Bishops, 1800–1850', *Historical Journal*, vol. xviii, no. 1, pp. 37–53, on which this chapter draws to a considerable extent.
2 A. de Tocqueville, *Journeys to England and Ireland* (London, 1957), ed. J. P. Mayer, p. 130.
3 *Freeman's Journal*, 10 April 1918. The members of the standing committee were Cardinal Logue, Archbishops Walsh (Dublin) and Harty (Cashel), and Bishops O'Donnell (Raphoe), O'Dea (Galway), Kelly (Ross), Browne (Cloyne), Foley (Kildare and Leighlin) and McRory (Dromore).
4 Wyse, *Late Catholic Association of Ireland*, Vol. i, p. 238.
5 *Dublin Evening Post*, 18 October 1834.
6 J. F. Broderick, *The Holy See and the Irish Movement for the Repeal of the Union with England* (Rome, 1951), pp. 58–9.
7 *The Times*, 13 January 1845.
8 *Pilot*, 15 January 1845.
9 *Pilot*, 24 January 1845.

10 J. H. Whyte, quoting Propaganda Archives, Acta, 1851, in P. J. Corish (ed.), *A History of Irish Catholicism* (Dublin, 1967), Vol. vi, pp. 8–9.

11 J. P. P. O'Shea, 'The Priest and Politics in County Tipperary 1850–1891' (Ph.D. thesis: NUI, 1979), p. 197. I am indebted to Dr O'Shea's work for several references in this section.

12 *Freeman's Journal*, 16 May 1881. Later in the same year, Croke went still further in this form of ambiguity in a speech at Wexford, 'No victory has ever been achieved without the loss of some valuable lives. You cannot make omelettes, as the French say, without breaking eggs', ibid., 10 October 1881.

13 *Tipperary Advocate*, 26 November 1887, quoted in O'Shea, 'Priest and Politics', p. 299.

14 ibid.

15 A. M. Sullivan, *New Ireland: Political Sketches and Personal Reminiscences* (London, 1878), Vol. ii, p. 203.

16 *Dublin Review*, April 1869, pp. 494–5.

17 *Freeman's Journal*, 2 January 1887.

18 ibid., 24 January 1878.

19 Croke to Archbishop Cullen, 25 January 1878, Cullen Papers, quoted in M. Tierney, *Croke of Cashel: the Life of Archbishop Thomas William Croke, 1823–1902* (Dublin, 1976), p. 91.

20 Croke to Cullen, Cullen Papers, 28 April 1878, quoted in Tierney, *Croke of Cashel*, p. 93.

21 Croke to Cullen, Cullen Papers, 10 May 1878, quoted in Tierney, *Croke of Cashel*, pp. 93–4.

22 *Flag of Ireland*, 2 March 1878, quoted in Tierney, *Croke of Cashel*, pp. 91–2.

Chapter 7

1 W. Arthur, *The Life of Gideon Ouseley* (London, 1876), p. 159, quoted in D. Bowen, *The Protestant Crusade in Ireland, 1800–70* (Dublin, 1978), p. 36.

2 D. Greene, 'The Irish Language Movement', in M. Hurley (ed.), *Irish Anglicanism, 1869–1969* (Dublin, 1970), p. 111.

3 F. Grannell, 'Early Irish Ecclesiastical Studies', in ibid., p. 49.

4 E. Curtis and R. B. McDowell (eds), *Irish Historical Documents* (London, 1943), pp. 311–13.

5 Maureen Wall, 'The Decline of the Irish Language', in B. O Cuiv (ed.), *A View of the Irish Language* (Dublin, 1969), p. 86.

6 F. S. L. Lyons, *Culture and Anarchy in Ireland 1890–1939* (Oxford, 1979), pp. 29–30.

7 T. W. Rolleston (ed.), *Prose Writings of Thomas Davis*, (London, n.d.), p. 160.

8 ibid., p. 193.

9 ibid., p. 160.

10 ibid., p. 164.

11 T. O. hAilin, 'Irish Revival Movements', in O Cuiv (ed.), *Irish Language*, p. 96.

12 *United Ireland*, 27 December 1884, quoted in Tierney, *Croke of Cashel*, p. 195.

13 Greene, 'Irish Language Movement', in Hurley (ed.), *Irish Anglicanism*, p. 115; George Moore, *Vale* (London, 1914), p. 249.

14 D. P. Moran, *The Philosophy of Irish Ireland* (Dublin, n.d.), p. 37.

15 D. G. Boyce, *Nationalism in Ireland* (London, 1982), p. 243.

16 K. Kroeber, 'Pride and Prejudice: Fiction's lasting Novelty?', in J. Halperin (ed.), *Jane Austen: Bi-centenary Essays* (Cambridge, 1975), p. 150.

17 T. Fiaich, 'The Language and Political History', in O Cuiv (ed.), *Irish Language*, p. 201.

18 Report of *Coimisuin na Gaeltachta* [R23/27], p. 3. See generally M. O'Callaghan, 'Land and Religion: the Quest for Identity in the Irish Free State, 1922–32' (unpublished MA dissertation: University College, Dublin, 1981).

19 S. O Cathain, 'Education in the New Ireland', in MacManus, (ed.), *Years of the Great Test*, p. 110.

20 ibid., pp. 109–10.

21 Report of the Department of Education for the year 1928–9, quoted in ibid., pp. 111–12.

22 'It is remarkable that any suggestion or request made by teachers, parents, members of the Oireachtas or other representative bodies or persons, for an impartial inquiry or investigation into the methods of teaching Irish in the schools, was invariably met with almost hysterical opposition by people who affected to believe that the request for investigation was an attack on the language itself', T. J. O'Connell, *History of the Irish National Teachers Organization* (Dublin, 1968), p. 373.

Chapter 8

1 E. M. Johnston, *Ireland in the Eighteenth Century* (Dublin, 1974), p. 42.

2 *Hansard*, new series, xiii, cols 98–9, 21 April 1825.

3 Johnston, *Ireland in the Eighteenth Century*, p. 175.

4 W. E. H. Lecky, *A History of Ireland in the Eighteenth Century*, (new edn: London, 1892), Vol. iv, p. 47.

5 ibid., Vol. iii, p. 94.

6 ibid., p. 98.

7 D. Gwynn, *The History of Partition, 1912–1925* (Dublin, 1950), p. 214.

8 *Hansard*, 5th series, cxlix, col. 40, 14 December 1921.

Index